# PRESIDENTS

*OF THE*

## United States

★ ★ ★ ★ ★

# TIME
## FOR KIDS

Editor, TIME For Kids: Nellie Gonzalez Cutler
Senior Editor, TIME For Kids: Brenda Iasevoli

# LIBERTY
## STREET

Executive Editor: Beth Sutinis
Project Editor: Nicole Fisher
Art Director: Georgia Morrissey
Designer: Laura Klynstra
Production Manager: Hillary Leary
Associate Prepress Manager: Alex Voznesenskiy

Published by Liberty Street, an imprint of Time Inc. Books
225 Liberty Street
New York, New York 10281

LIBERTY STREET and TIME FOR KIDS are trademarks of
Time Inc.

ISBN: 978-1-68330-000-7
Library of Congress Control Number: 2016955036

First edition, 2017

1 QGT 16

10 9 8 7 6 5 4 3 2 1

Time Inc. Books products may be purchased for business or
promotional use. For information on bulk purchases, please
contact Christi Crowley in the Special Sales Department at
(845) 895-9858.

To order Time Inc. Books Collector's Editions, please call
(800) 327-6388, Monday through Friday, 7 a.m.-9 p.m., Central
Time.

We welcome your comments and suggestions about Time Inc.
Books.
Please write to us at:
Time Inc. Books

Attention: Book Editors

P.O. Box 62310
Tampa, Florida 33662-2310

timeincbooks.com

FOR KIDS

# PRESIDENTS

## OF THE

# United States

# CONTENTS

The Signing of the
Constitution of the United States.

# The Story of the Presidency

In 1787, America's founding fathers faced an enormous task. They had to create a strong government for the new country. Representatives from each of the states, called delegates, met in Philadelphia. General George Washington was asked to lead the meeting, which later became known as the Constitutional Convention. He had directed the military during the country's successful war for independence from Great Britain. And he was the new nation's first great hero.

The war had ended four years earlier. During those four years, the Articles of Confederation governed the former colonies. This document provided direction to the new states but only loosely tied them together as a nation. The delegates fixed this problem when they wrote the Constitution, which called for a strong central government.

## LEADING A NATION

The delegates had different ideas about how powerful the country's leaders should be. They had not liked being ruled by England's all-powerful king. Some even argued that America should have several top leaders, not just one, to make sure that no single leader ever became as powerful as a king. While the delegates finally agreed to have one person head the nation, they made sure to create a system that would check, or control, the power of the leader.

The delegates also struggled with how long the leader should serve. Some felt one long term, of up to seven years, would be best. Others felt short terms would be better. The delegates came to agree that the leader could serve a four-year term and could run for reelection when the term ended.

## A POWERFUL POSITION

By the end of the convention, the delegates had outlined the powers of the nation's top leader. These powers included serving as the head of the military, making agreements with other nations, and choosing people to hold important government jobs. In 1788, the method of election differed by state. In some states the public voted, and in others the state lawmakers voted. But people who represented the states, called the electoral college, cast the final votes.

Federal Hall in New York City was home to the new nation's government.

On April 30, 1789, George Washington became the first person elected to the highest office in the land. After the election, people debated what to call him. Some ideas were "His Elective Majesty" and even "His Highness, the President of the United States and Protector of the Rights of the Same." The final decision was to use the simple title "President of the United States."

On April 30, 1789, Washington stood on the balcony of Federal Hall in New York City and recited the presidential oath of office.

# The Three Branches of Government

The writers of the Constitution wanted to create a very strong national government. But they also wanted to make sure that one person or group did not have too much power. Their solution was to separate the government's powers into three parts called the legislative, executive, and judicial branches. Each branch of government can limit the powers of the others. This way no branch becomes too powerful.

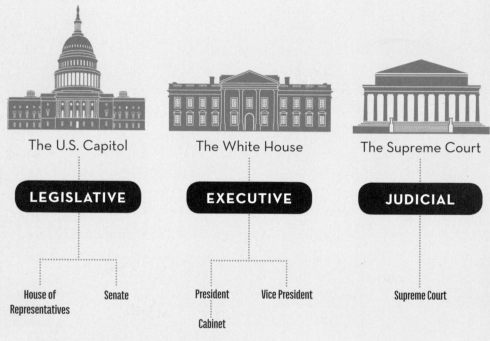

The U.S. Capitol

The White House

The Supreme Court

**LEGISLATIVE**

**EXECUTIVE**

**JUDICIAL**

House of Representatives

Senate

President

Vice President

Cabinet

Supreme Court

Did You Know?

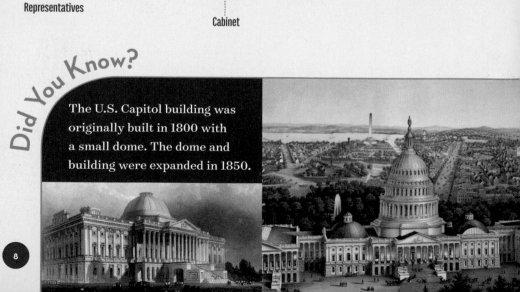

The U.S. Capitol building was originally built in 1800 with a small dome. The dome and building were expanded in 1850.

## LEGISLATIVE

The legislative branch includes the two houses of Congress—the Senate and the House of Representatives. There are 100 senators and 435 representatives who are elected by the people. Members of Congress write bills and then vote on whether the bills should become laws. They decide how the federal budget will be spent. And

The Capitol Building is home to the United States Congress.

the legislative branch also votes before the U.S. can go to war with another country. Senators serve in office for six-year terms. Representatives serve two-year terms.

The president and his staff work at the White House.

## EXECUTIVE

The president is the head of the executive branch. This branch also includes the vice president and the cabinet, a group of the president's close advisors. The president signs bills into laws. The president may also veto, or reject, bills. But Congress can take a vote to cancel a president's veto. This is called an override. The president chooses cabinet members and Supreme Court judges, but the Senate must approve the president's choices. The president is also commander-in-chief of the armed forces and can serve up to two four-year terms in office.

## JUDICIAL

The Supreme Court is the head of the judicial branch. It is the most powerful court in the country. Its nine justices, or judges, decide if laws agree with the Constitution. Once justices are approved to serve on the Supreme Court, they can stay on the court for the rest of their lives.

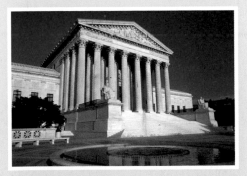

The Supreme Court decides cases at the Supreme Court Building in Washington, D.C.

# Why Do We Have Political Parties?

A political party is a group of people in government who work to get candidates elected. People who join a party share the same general ideas about what government should do and how it should do it.

Today we have two main political parties in the United States—the Democrats and the Republicans. This two-party system has been in place since about 1869.

Some voters don't want to be associated with either party. These voters are considered independent and do not vote in primary elections.

## DEMOCRATIC PARTY PLATFORM

★ A strong federal government is best.
★ The government should take an active role in providing for citizens, especially those in need.
★ Taxes should be high enough to pay for government programs.
★ Businesses and the economy should be regulated by law.

## REPUBLICAN PARTY PLATFORM

★ The individual states should have more power than the federal government.
★ The government should not play a large role in the lives of citizens.
★ Taxes should be lower and the government should be smaller overall.
★ Businesses and the economy should mostly be left to run themselves.

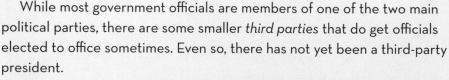

While most government officials are members of one of the two main political parties, there are some smaller *third parties* that do get officials elected to office sometimes. Even so, there has not yet been a third-party president.

One third party is the Libertarian Party, which believes government should only intervene in the lives of citizens to help individuals guard against force or fraud. Another is the Green Party, which supports grassroots democracy (the idea of empowering regular people). The Green Party aims to protect the environment and consider environmental impacts before making any decisions.

# POLITICAL PARTIES OF THE PAST

Throughout American history, political parties have come and gone. In fact, many early presidents belonged to political parties that no longer exist. Here are a few important ones.

| | | |
|---|---|---|
| **FEDERALIST PARTY**<br>Ideas: National bank, strong central government, tariff system, strong ties to Britain | Founded by: Alexander Hamilton<br><br>Dates in existence: 1789–1824 |  |
| **DEMOCRATIC-REPUBLICAN PARTY**<br>Ideas: Strong state governments, support of farming economy, strict adherence to the Constitution | Founded by: Thomas Jefferson<br><br>Dates in existence: 1799–1828 |  |
| **WHIG PARTY**<br>Ideas: Strong tariffs, increase federal spending to modernize the country, opposition to a powerful presidency | Founded by: Henry Clay<br><br>Dates in existence: 1833–1854 | |

Political cartoon: President Theodore Roosevelt giving the Republican elephant a spoonful of "Trust Legislation Tonic."

# George Washington ★

**1789 to 1797**

## 1ST PRESIDENT

**BORN:** February 22, 1732, in Westmoreland County, VA

**DIED:** December 14, 1799, at Mount Vernon, VA

**POLITICAL PARTY:** Federalist

**VICE PRESIDENT:** John Adams

**WIFE:** Martha Dandridge Custis

**STEPCHILDREN:** John, Martha

Martha Washington

George Washington was a well-respected hero of the American Revolution and is called the "father of our country."

Washington came from a successful farming family in Virginia. As a young man, he was a plantation owner and surveyor. He served with the British army during the French and Indian Wars. He also participated in Virginia's colonial government.

The 1770s were a time of change in Britain's American colonies. The colonists felt they had no voice in Britain and were being taxed unfairly on British goods. Starting in 1775, leaders from the 13 colonies gathered in Philadelphia to discuss whether to take action against the king. George Washington attended the First and Second Continental Congresses and took command of the newly established colonial army. In the eyes of King George III and the British, he was now a traitor.

A year later, the colonial congress adopted a Declaration of Independence from Britain. The new nation was to be called the United States. Washington's U.S. army wasn't well trained. His soldiers didn't have enough supplies. But Washington was a smart leader. And the new nation's army got help from the French. The French were happy to fight against Britain, their enemy.

In April 1783, following nearly six years of war, the Americans won their freedom

> "Liberty, when it begins to take root, is a plant of rapid growth."
> —George Washington

★ ★ ★ ★

when the British gave up all claims to the former colonies.

General Washington returned to a quiet life at his Virginia plantation, Mount Vernon. But the quiet didn't last long.

After the war, weak laws called the Articles of Confederation held together the new United States of America. In 1787, state leaders met in Philadelphia to draft a new Constitution. This plan emphasized the importance of a strong central government to help the states work together. And in June 1788, the states approved a new Constitution. This document became the foundation of American government.

Washington was elected president of the new nation at the meeting in Philadelphia. In a world of kings and queens, Washington proved that a president chosen by the people could be a strong leader. He died two years after he completed two terms as president. Congressman Henry Lee said he was "first in war, first in peace, and first in the hearts of his countrymen."

**Washington reviewing the Western Army at Fort Cumberland, Maryland**

## KEY DATES

**1789:** French Revolution begins.

**1790:** U.S. Supreme Court meets for the first time. First U.S. census counts nearly four million people.

**1791:** First ten amendments to the Constitution are approved (Bill of Rights).

**1793:** Eli Whitney invents the cotton gin, which removes seeds from cotton fiber quickly.

**1795:** Metric system is introduced in France.

### Did You Know?

Washington's farewell speech is read aloud in the Senate every year.

# John Adams

**1797 to 1801**

## 2ND PRESIDENT

**BORN:** October 30, 1735, in Braintree (now Quincy), MA

**DIED:** July 4, 1826, in Quincy, MA

**POLITICAL PARTY:** Federalist

**VICE PRESIDENT:** Thomas Jefferson

**WIFE:** Abigail Smith

**CHILDREN:** Abigail, John Quincy, Susanna, Charles, Thomas Boylston

Peacefield or Old House, the home of John Adams

The son of a town councilman, John Adams was always in the thick of the action. He attended Harvard University and became a lawyer in Massachusetts. In 1774, he was elected to the Massachusetts General Assembly. He became a leader in the fight for America's independence, attending the First Continental Congress and working with Thomas Jefferson on the wording of the Declaration of Independence. He served as a diplomat for the colonies, spending nearly 10 years in Europe. And then he became the country's first vice president, a position that he described as an "insignificant office" because he did not have enough to do.

In 1796, Adams beat Thomas Jefferson in the race for president. At the time, France and Britain were fighting. Like Washington before him, Adams wanted the U.S. to avoid taking sides in the war. But American shipping was suffering.

Following attacks on U.S. ships by the French in 1798, Adams expanded the army, asking George Washington to lead it once again. He also created the U.S. Navy to defend American ships at sea. Adams sent diplomats to France for peace talks. Three French officials, known as X, Y, and Z, told the Americans that there would be no talks until the U.S. paid a bribe. When this story got out, many angry Americans wanted war. The scandal became known as the XYZ Affair.

In 1800, Adams sent more diplomats to France. This time they were successful, and a peace treaty was signed. Adams was proud that he had kept the U.S. out of war.

But his reputation had been seriously damaged by the passage of the Alien and Sedition Acts in 1798. Designed to limit the power of the Democrat-Republicans, the acts allowed the president to deport or imprison non-citizens from a hostile nation or who were considered "dangerous to the peace and safety of the United States." The acts also made it more difficult to become a citizen, and created penalties for publishing false statements that were critical of the government. Although Adams did not write the acts, they were created by his fellow Federalists, and Adams signed them into law.

In November of 1801, he moved into the newly constructed White House, becoming the first president to live there. But he would not stay for long. When he ran again for president that year, Thomas Jefferson defeated him.

Adams retired to his farm in Massachusetts. As time passed, Adams and his rival Jefferson became close friends. They wrote dozens of letters to each other, discussing religion, government, and philosophy. Adams died on July 4, 1826, just hours after Jefferson died in Virginia.

Adams's wife, Abigail, was his most important advisor.

## KEY DATES

**1798:** French Emperor Napoléon Bonaparte conquers Rome and Egypt for France.

**1800:** The U.S. capital moves from Philadelphia to Washington, D.C. The U.S. Library of Congress is founded.

**1801:** The United Kingdom of Great Britain and Ireland is established with one monarch and one parliament.

### Did You Know?

Adams established the U.S. Navy and ordered the first warships to be built.

# Thomas Jefferson

**·1801 to 1809**

## 3RD PRESIDENT

**BORN:** April 13, 1743, in Albemarle County, VA

**DIED:** July 4, 1826, in Charlottesville, VA

**POLITICAL PARTY:** Democratic-Republican

**VICE PRESIDENTS:** Aaron Burr, George Clinton

**WIFE:** Martha Wayles Skelton

**CHILDREN:** Martha, Mary, Lucy, Elizabeth*

*Three other children died in infancy.

Martha Jefferson

Thomas Jefferson grew up in a wealthy plantation family. Taught by private tutors, his education was better than most others' in the mid-1700s. He was a great thinker, architect, inventor, farmer, and patriot. Yet this tall man with a face full of freckles was more comfortable writing down his thoughts than speaking in public. When it came time for the colonies to break away from Britain, Jefferson was asked to write the Declaration of Independence.

After the Revolutionary War, when the colonies became free, Jefferson was appointed America's ambassador to France. Several years passed and Jefferson wanted to return to Monticello, his Virginia home, to write and farm. But when George Washington became president, he asked Jefferson to be secretary of state—the person in charge of managing foreign affairs.

His country continued to need him, and in 1796, Jefferson was elected vice president. Four years later, he beat John Adams, the incumbent, in the race for the presidency. During his first term, Jefferson made an important decision to expand the United States territory. In 1803, he bought a huge area of land from France. The Louisiana Purchase just about doubled the size of the nation.

Jefferson sent Meriwether Lewis and William Clark to explore the new territory. The men, along with others on their team, traveled all the way to the Pacific coast. The group returned in 1806 with important information about the areas in the western part of the continent.

After two terms as president, Jefferson went back to Monticello. He helped start up the University of Virginia in 1819. And he continued to write until his death on July 4, 1826—50 years after he wrote the Declaration of Independence.

While Jefferson was much beloved, his legacy is not simple. Although he wrote often about the need to abolish slavery, he himself owned as many as 600 slaves in his lifetime.

Benjamin Franklin and John Adams helped Jefferson write the Declaration of Independence.

# KEY DATES

**1804:** Lewis and Clark begin their journey west on the Missouri River.

**1805:** Jefferson takes the oath of office to begin his second term.

**1807:** Robert Fulton makes the first steamboat trip, going from New York City to Albany, NY.

**1808:** Beethoven's Fifth and Sixth Symponies are performed for the first time.

## Did You Know?

It was Jefferson's idea to create U.S. money on a decimal system with the dollar, or 100 cents, as the base.

# James Madison

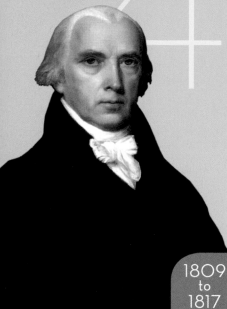

1809 to 1817

## 4TH PRESIDENT

**BORN:** March 16, 1751, in Port Conway, VA

**DIED:** June 28, 1836, at Montpelier, VA

**POLITICAL PARTY:** Democratic-Republican

**VICE PRESIDENTS:** George Clinton, Elbridge Gerry

**WIFE:** Dolley Payne Todd

**CHILDREN:** stepson John Payne Todd

James Madison, the son of a Virginia plantation owner, was a small man who was often sick. He felt that he was too weak to hold an important job. But Madison was a strong thinker and expert on British laws. When the American colonies finally broke away from Britain, Madison knew that the new country would need a government strong enough to protect people's rights, but not so strong that it could take away people's freedom. He was just the person to help. He wrote many parts of the new U.S. Constitution, including what became the Bill of Rights. Then he did something even more difficult: he helped persuade people to accept it.

Madison served as secretary of state when Thomas Jefferson was president.

When Madison was elected president, in 1809, France and Britain were still fighting a war. The U.S. was caught in the middle. When the British attacked American ships, Madison felt it was time to fight back. The War of 1812 lasted about two years. In the end, the war was seen as an American victory, and Madison left office as a popular president.

> "The truth is that all men having power ought to be mistrusted."
> —James Madison

## KEY DATES

**1811:** The largest series of earthquakes known in North America happens in the Mississippi River Valley.

**1812:** Napoléon, emperor of France, invades Russia and loses 600,000 soldiers.

# James Monroe

1817 to 1825

James Monroe was a Virginia college student in the early days of the American Revolution. He wanted to help, so he joined Washington's army.

When Thomas Jefferson was president, he sent Monroe to France to discuss the territory called Louisiana. This was a huge piece of land in North America that the French controlled. Monroe helped Jefferson buy the land in the Louisiana Purchase.

Monroe had been governor of Virginia, a U.S. senator, and a diplomat to Britain and to France. He had also served as Madison's secretary of state and secretary of war. When he ran for president, he won easily.

When Monroe was president, more changes to the U.S. took place. On the western edge of the nation, Missouri wanted to enter the union as a slave state. This was controversial. Finally, in 1820, an agreement was reached, called the Missouri Compromise. It allowed Maine to enter as a free state and Missouri as a slaveholding state.

In 1819, Monroe agreed to purchase Florida from Spain. Then, in 1823, he made a very important speech. He said that the countries of Europe must keep out of the affairs of the independent nations and colonies in North and South America. This idea became known as the Monroe Doctrine.

## 5TH PRESIDENT

**BORN:** April 28, 1758, in Westmoreland County, VA

**DIED:** July 4, 1831, in New York City, NY

**POLITICAL PARTY:** Democratic-Republican

**VICE PRESIDENT:** Daniel D. Tompkins

**WIFE:** Elizabeth Kortright

**CHILDREN:** James Spence, Maria Hester*

*One other child died in infancy.

**1814:** Francis Scott Key writes a poem that will be adapted into "The Star-Spangled Banner."

**1819:** Simón Bolívar leads wars for independence throughout South America.

**1821:** Mexico declares independence from Spain.

# John Quincy Adams

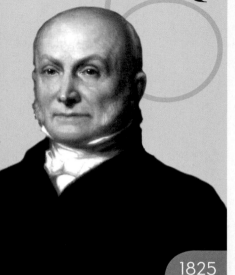

1825 to 1829

## 6TH PRESIDENT

**BORN:** July 11, 1767, in Quincy, MA

**DIED:** February 23, 1848, in Washington, D.C.

**POLITICAL PARTY:** Democratic-Republican

**VICE PRESIDENT:** John C. Calhoun

**WIFE:** Louisa Catherine Johnson

**CHILDREN:** George Washington, John, Charles Francis, Louisa

As the son of the second president, John Quincy Adams had a close look at the life of a political leader and diplomat. In his career, he was both.

Adams was seven when the American Revolution began. As a teenager, he traveled to Europe with his father who represented the new U.S. John Quincy was appointed Minister to the Netherlands in 1794, and served as minister to several European countries from then until 1817.

Adams formed opinions while in Europe about the role the U.S. should play in the world. He saw how nations pulled one another into war and thought the U.S. should never take the side of one nation.

Back in the U.S., Adams was appointed secretary of state under President Monroe. In 1824, Adams ran for president. Andrew Jackson got more votes, but the election was very close, and neither candidate got enough electoral votes. The House of Representatives had to pick a winner. They chose Adams.

In the next election, Jackson won. Adams is often said to have been the smartest man to ever hold the office of president. He served in Congress until his death in 1848 and helped create the museum that would later be called the Smithsonian Institution.

## KEY DATES

**1827:** First black newspaper, *Freedom's Journal*, begins publishing.

**1828:** Construction begins on the first public railroad in the U.S. (B&O Railroad).

# Andrew Jackson

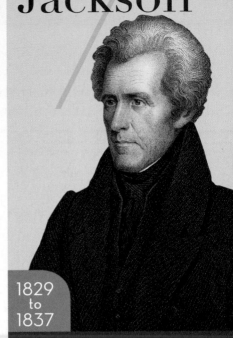

Andrew Jackson was born in a log cabin. Both his parents had died by the time he was 14. He didn't have a lot of formal schooling.

As a young man, Jackson studied law and traded furs. Later he bought a plantation in Tennessee, where he kept slaves. But Jackson was still known as a man of the people. He believed that common citizens should run the country and thought government should be simple and straightforward.

During the War of 1812, Jackson was a major general. He led his men to victory against the British at New Orleans. He ran for president in 1824 and got more votes than John Quincy Adams. But he lost when the House of Representatives decided the close election. In 1828, Jackson ran again and won.

Jackson was a powerful president. He fought with Congress and disagreed with laws that he thought favored the wealthy. Some people thought he was too forceful. They called him King Andrew.

He also worked to remove American Indian tribes from their land. Thousands of Indians died traveling the "Trail of Tears" from their ancestral lands in the east to what is now Oklahoma.

After two terms as president, Jackson retired. But he continued to give advice to the new president, Martin Van Buren.

**1829 to 1837**

## 7TH PRESIDENT

**BORN:** March 15, 1767, in The Waxhaws, SC

**DIED:** June 8, 1845, in Nashville, TN

**POLITICAL PARTY:** Democratic

**VICE PRESIDENTS:** John C. Calhoun, Martin Van Buren

**WIFE:** Rachel Donelson

**CHILDREN:** adopted nephew Andrew Jr., guardian to six other children.

**1829:** At the age of twenty, Louis Braille develops a system of six dots to help the blind read.

**1830:** Jackson signs the Indian Removal Act, which requires American Indians to move west to the frontier.

**1836:** Texas declares independence from Mexico. The Mexican army wins Battle at the Alamo.

# Go West, Young America!

In the 150 years following the American Revolution, the United States grew to three times its original size. The presidents played a big role, from making deals with other heads of state to waging war to seize territory by force. Sometimes, others in government made the deals and the presidents supported them.

The map on the right shows when big pieces of land, called territories, were added to the U.S., and who was president when the territory was added.

The United States is unique in how it added to its territory. Most other countries' basic borders were established before their current government took power. The expansion of the U.S. has played a large role in how Americans view the nation and its people—often as pioneers fulfilling a destiny to have the country stretch from one ocean to another.

This expansion came at a great and terrible price, though. What the map doesn't show is where territory was seized from American Indian tribes through treaty agreements, armed conflict, or forced takeover and occupation. Historians estimate that the population of native peoples in what is now the United States might have been as high as 100 million people before Europeans came to North America. The population of American Indians and native Alaskans is now around 5.2 million.

Settlers fighting American Indians in the Battle of the Thames in the 1800s.

# From Sea to Shining Sea

This map shows when the U.S. acquired land from other nations, and who was president at the time. (It doesn't show when land was acquired through treaty agreements, wars, or takeovers from American Indian nations.)

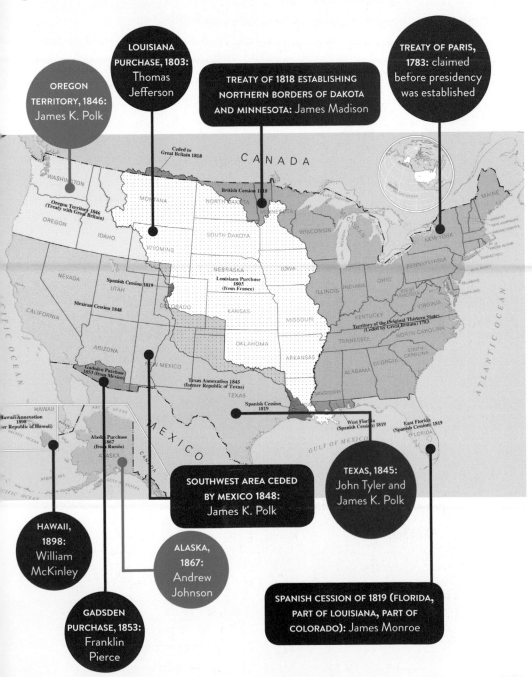

OREGON TERRITORY, 1846: James K. Polk

LOUISIANA PURCHASE, 1803: Thomas Jefferson

TREATY OF 1818 ESTABLISHING NORTHERN BORDERS OF DAKOTA AND MINNESOTA: James Madison

TREATY OF PARIS, 1783: claimed before presidency was established

HAWAII, 1898: William McKinley

GADSDEN PURCHASE, 1853: Franklin Pierce

ALASKA, 1867: Andrew Johnson

SOUTHWEST AREA CEDED BY MEXICO 1848: James K. Polk

TEXAS, 1845: John Tyler and James K. Polk

SPANISH CESSION OF 1819 (FLORIDA, PART OF LOUISIANA, PART OF COLORADO): James Monroe

# Martin Van Buren  ★

1837
to
1841

## 8TH PRESIDENT

**BORN:** December 5, 1782, in Kinderhook, NY

**DIED:** July 24, 1862, in Kinderhook, NY

**POLITICAL PARTY:** Democratic

**VICE PRESIDENT:** Richard M. Johnson

**WIFE:** Hannah Hoes

**CHILDREN:** Abraham, John, Martin Jr., Smith*

*One other child died in infancy.

Martin Van Buren had the nickname "the Little Magician." He was a friendly, cheerful politician who knew how to work with people and get things done.

> "As to the presidency, the two happiest days of my life were those of my entrance upon the office and my surrender of it."
>
> —Martin Van Buren

Van Buren was born in 1782 in Kinderhook, New York. He was the first president who did not start life as a British subject.

Van Buren worked for an attorney and learned law. Later, he became a New York City lawyer.

Over his career, Van Buren was a state senator, a U.S. senator, and New York's governor. Van Buren also became a big supporter of Andrew Jackson.

Van Buren was President Jackson's secretary of state and then vice president during Jackson's second term. With Jackson's support, Van Buren was elected president in 1836. But there was some big trouble waiting.

As president, Jackson had put the Bank of the United States out of business. Shortly after Van Buren became president, banks all over the country failed. Many people lost their jobs. Voters blamed the new president for the bad times. When Van Buren ran again, he lost.

## KEY DATES

**1837:** Victoria becomes queen of Great Britain.

**1838:** More than 15,000 Cherokees are forced to walk from Georgia to Indian Territory. About 4,000 die.

**1839:** West African slaves take control of the Cuban slave ship *Amistad*.

# William Henry Harrison

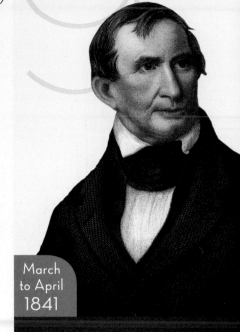

In the early 1800s, Native Americans were forced off their land to make way for white settlers. When tribes resisted, the Army intervened. William Henry Harrison made a name for himself fighting Native Americans who were defending their way of life.

In 1811, he won a battle against the Shawnee tribe in Indiana, near a river called Tippecanoe. From the battle, he got the nickname "Tippecanoe," which became part of his 1840 presidential campaign slogan, "Tippecanoe and Tyler, too." (John Tyler was his running mate.)

Like many earlier presidents, Harrison was from Virginia. He began studying to be a doctor but joined the army to earn a living. For the rest of his life, he divided his time between the army and politics.

As a war hero, Harrison was popular with voters. After he settled in Ohio, he became a state senator, a U.S. representative, a U.S. senator, governor of the Indiana Territory, and minister to Colombia in South America. He first ran for president in 1836 against Martin Van Buren and lost. In 1840, he was elected.

At his inauguration in March 1841, Harrison gave a long speech outdoors on a cold, wet day. Soon after, he became ill with pneumonia. He died 31 days later. He was the first president to die in office.

## March to April 1841

## 9TH PRESIDENT

**BORN:** February 9, 1773, in Carles City County, VA

**DIED:** April 4, 1841, in Washington, D.C.

**POLITICAL PARTY:** Whig

**VICE PRESIDENT:** John Tyler

**WIFE:** Anna Tuthill Symmes

**CHILDREN:** Elizabeth, John, Lucy, William, John Scott, Mary, Carter, Anna, James*

*One other child died in infancy.

**1841:** Twenty-six states make up the U.S., and the population reaches 17 million.

**1841:** Adolphe Sax invents the saxophone in Belgium.

# John Tyler

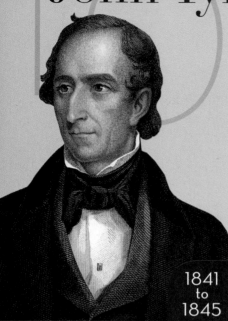

**1841 to 1845**

## 10TH PRESIDENT

**BORN:** March 29, 1790, in Charles City County, VA

**DIED:** January 18, 1862, in Richmond, VA

**POLITICAL PARTY:** Whig

**VICE PRESIDENT:** None

**WIVES:** Letitia Christian, Julia Gardiner

**CHILDREN:** Mary, Robert, John Jr., Letitia, Elizabeth, Anne, Alice, Tazewell, David, John Alexander, Julia, Lachlan, Lyon, Robert Fitzwalter, Pearl

The U.S. Constitution now says that if a president dies, "the Powers and Duties of [the] Office shall [pass to] the Vice President." When President Harrison died, it wasn't that clear. Vice President John Tyler needed to decide his next steps. He assumed the role of president and started asserting his power. Tyler was from a wealthy Virginia family. He had been a U.S. representative, a governor, and a U.S. senator. He felt he was ready to lead the country.

As vice president, Tyler was popular with the southern voters, but no one had expected him to be in charge of the whole country. Many congressmen made it difficult for President Tyler. They worked against him, and even impeached him in 1842. Eventually, they threw him out of the Whig Party, which made it hard for him to run for election in 1844.

But Tyler kept pushing for things he believed in. He fought to make it easier for settlers to get land in the West. He also got approval from Congress to claim Texas for the U. S.

When the Civil War began in 1861, Tyler was elected to the Confederate Congress of the southern states trying to break free from the Union. Because of this, Tyler is the only president ever to be named an enemy of the U.S.

## KEY DATES

**1842:** Ether is used in surgery for the first time to eliminate pain.

**1843:** Samuel Morse patents the telegraph.

**1845:** Edgar Allan Poe publishes *The Raven and Other Poems.* Game rules for baseball are established.

# James K. Polk

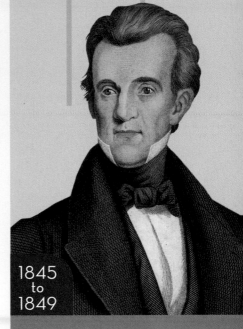

Although James Knox Polk was known to politics in the mid-1840s, it was still a surprise when he ran for president. Originally from North Carolina, he had been a lawyer in Tennessee and served in state government. Then Polk became a U.S. representative and, later, governor of Tennessee.

In 1844, Polk supported letting Texas into the Union. But by entering the Union as a slaveholding state, Texas would upset the balance of power in Congress. Polk proposed acquiring the Oregon Territory as a free territory, which would maintain the balance between free and slaveholding states.

In 1846, there was a disagreement over borders in Texas, and Polk sent troops. This led to war in Mexico, which cost thousands of lives. The war was successful, and the U.S. gained the territory from New Mexico to California. Polk then negotiated with Britain for control of the Oregon Territory, which included Oregon, Idaho, Washington, and parts of Montana and Wyoming.

Polk had delivered on his campaign promises. But more important, when he left office, he left a country that stretched all the way from the Atlantic Ocean to the Pacific. The new lands were rich with resources, including gold, silver, and—it would one day be discovered—oil and natural gas.

**1845 to 1849**

## 11TH PRESIDENT

**BORN:** November 2, 1795, in Mecklenburg County, NC

**DIED:** June 15, 1849, in Nashville, TN

**POLITICAL PARTY:** Democratic

**VICE PRESIDENT:** George M. Dallas

**WIFE:** Sarah Childress

**CHILDREN:** None

**1846:** U.S. declares war against Mexico. Failure of potato crop causes famine in Ireland.

**1848:** Gold is discovered at Sutter's Mill in California. War in Mexico ends.

# Zachary Taylor

1849 to 1850

## 12TH PRESIDENT

**BORN:** November 24, 1784, in Montebello, VA

**DIED:** July 9, 1850, in Washington, D.C.

**POLITICAL PARTY:** Whig

**VICE PRESIDENT:** Millard Fillmore

**WIFE:** Margaret Mackall Smith

**CHILDREN:** Ann, Sarah Knox, Octavia, Margaret, Mary Elizabeth, Richard

Zachary Taylor had never worked in government when he ran for president. He didn't even vote in elections. But he was a national hero and the public loved him.

> "The idea that I should become president ... has never entered my head."
> —Zachary Taylor

Taylor was born in Montebello, Virginia, and grew up in Kentucky. He was a soldier. He fought in the War of 1812 and in battles against American Indian tribes. He was known for forcing white settlers to obey treaties the U.S. had made with American Indians. His role in the Mexican War made him a household name.

Taylor's soldiers gave him the nickname "Old Rough and Ready." He shared the hardships of his men. He usually didn't wear a uniform, and his clothes were often dirty.

As president, Taylor did things his own way. He was a slaveowner who was ready to go to war to keep the Union together. During his time in office, the 30 states were equally split between slaveholding and free states. Taylor urged Congress to admit California and New Mexico to the Union as free states.

On July 4, 1850, President Taylor became ill. He died a few days later. Taylor's presidency lasted only 16 months.

## KEY DATES

**1849:** The Gold Rush begins as thousands head to California seeking fortunes from gold.

**1849:** Elizabeth Blackwell of New York becomes first woman to receive a medical degree.

# Millard Fillmore

13

After Zachary Taylor died, Millard Fillmore became president. No one imagined he would be the leader of the nation.

> "An honorable defeat is better than a dishonorable victory."
> —Millard Fillmore

Born into a poor farm family in New York, Fillmore had barely any education. He worked on the farm. As a teen, he trained to be a cloth maker. But Fillmore wanted to learn to read and write. Soon he found a tutor, Abigail, whom he later married.

Before becoming Taylor's vice president, Fillmore served in New York state government and was a U.S. representative. As vice president, he often disagreed with President Taylor. Taylor was angered by threats from southern states to leave the nation; Fillmore wanted to keep southerners happy.

As president, Fillmore supported the Compromise of 1850. This let California enter the Union as a free state but allowed slavery in the new southwestern territories. The Compromise also ensured that slaves who escaped to freedom could be caught and returned to their slave holders.

At the next election in 1852, the Whig Party would not support him for president. Fillmore tried again to run for president in 1856 and was unsuccessful.

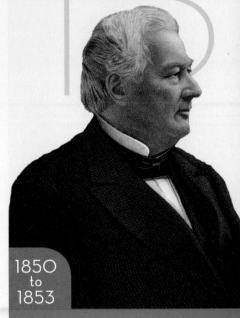

1850 to 1853

## 13TH PRESIDENT

**BORN:** Jan 7, 1800, in Summerhill, NY

**DIED:** March 8, 1874, in Buffalo, NY

**POLITICAL PARTY:** Whig

**VICE PRESIDENT:** None

**WIFE:** Abigail Powers

**CHILDREN:** Millard Powers, Mary Abigail

**1850:** California becomes the 31st state.

**1852:** Harriet Beecher Stowe publishes an anti-slavery novel called *Uncle Tom's Cabin*.

**1853:** Commodore Matthew Perry arrives in Japan to open trade with the nation.

# Franklin Pierce

1853 to 1857

## 14TH PRESIDENT

**BORN:** November 23, 1804, in Hillsboro, NH

**DIED:** October 8, 1869, in Concord, NH

**POLITICAL PARTY:** Democratic

**VICE PRESIDENT:** William R. King

**WIFE:** Jane Means Appleton

**CHILDREN:** Frank Robert, Benjamin*

*One other child died in infancy.

Franklin Pierce said that being president was "an impossible task to undertake in one term." He never had the chance for a second term.

Pierce, who was born and raised in New Hampshire, practiced law. Then he served in his state's government and in the U.S. Congress. In 1842, he gave up politics to please his wife, Jane, who disliked Washington, D.C. Four years later, Pierce fought in the Mexican War. After the war, he returned to his law practice.

As the 1852 presidential election drew to a close, Democrats could not agree on a candidate. They wanted to appeal to the largest number of voters and so chose a proslavery northerner—Pierce.

In early 1853, Pierce's son was killed in a train accident. After the inauguration, Vice President William R. King died of tuberculosis.

Pierce signed the Kansas-Nebraska Act, which undid the antislavery part of the Missouri Compromise of 1820. The act said that settlers in Kansas and Nebraska could choose to allow slavery. People for and against slavery fought for control of Kansas. These battles became known as Bleeding Kansas. As Pierce's term ended, the Democratic Party wouldn't support his reelection.

## KEY DATES

**1853:** Yellow fever kills 7,790 people in New Orleans.

**1854:** Republican Party is formed by antislavery northerners. Henry David Thoreau publishes *Walden*.

**1857:** The Panic of 1857—the first worldwide economic crisis—occurs.

# ★ James Buchanan

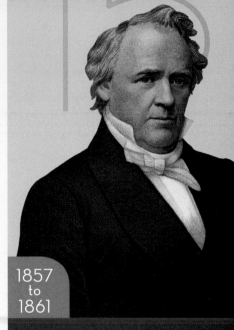

James Buchanan was a U.S. Senator from Pennsylvania and Secretary of State. As president, he inherited a country in conflict. Northerners wanted to stop the spread of slavery. Southerners wanted new states to be allowed to choose slavery.

Two days after Buchanan's term began, the Supreme Court made a landmark decision. A slave named Dred Scott, who was brought by his owner into free territory, sued his owner for freedom. The court ruled that slaves were property rather than citizens and could not sue.

Buchanan urged the nation to support the court's decision. This made northerners angry. Meanwhile, settlers in the Kansas Territory voted for a proslavery state constitution. Buchanan urged Congress to accept Kansas as a state that allowed slavery. Congress asked for a new constitution representing *all voters* in the territory. The new constitution rejected slavery. Many citizens believed Buchanan tried to sneak in Kansas as a proslavery state.

Before becoming president, James Buchanan had held public office and served as a diplomat in Russia and Britain. But as president, Buchanan wasn't able to bring the two sides of the nation together. He opted not to run for reelection in 1860.

## 1857 to 1861

## 15TH PRESIDENT

**BORN:** April 23, 1791, in Cove Gap, PA

**DIED:** June 1, 1868, in Lancaster, PA

**POLITICAL PARTY:** Democratic

**VICE PRESIDENT:** John C. Breckinridge

**WIFE:** None

**CHILDREN:** None

**1858:** First telegraph cable across the continent is completed, linking communication across the U.S.

**1861:** Confederate States of America is established; Jefferson Davis is elected president.

# Abraham Lincoln

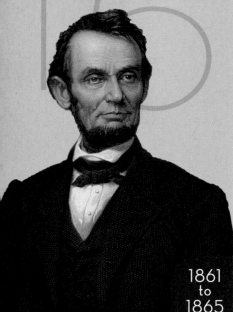

1861
to
1865

## 16TH PRESIDENT

**BORN:** February 12, 1809, in Hardin County, KY

**DIED:** April 15, 1865, in Washington, D.C.

**POLITICAL PARTY:** Republican

**VICE PRESIDENTS:** Hannibal Hamlin, Andrew Johnson

**WIFE:** Mary Todd

**CHILDREN:** Robert Todd, Edward, William Wallace, Thomas (Tad)

Mary Todd Lincoln

Abraham Lincoln took the helm of a nation broken apart. But by the end of his term, he had reunited the country. Lincoln was born in Kentucky to a poor pioneer family. He had almost no schooling but taught himself to read and write. As a young man, Lincoln became a lawyer and was elected to the Illinois state legislature and the U.S. House of Representatives.

> "Be sure you put your feet in the right place, then stand firm."
> —Abraham Lincoln

In 1858, Lincoln ran for the U.S. Senate. His opponent, Stephen A. Douglas, thought voters should decide if slavery should be allowed in new states. Lincoln publicly disagreed and said slavery must not be allowed to spread. Although Lincoln lost the 1858 election, he impressed many people. In one of the debates, he said: "A house divided against itself cannot stand." The house he was referring to was the United States.

Two years later, the country elected Lincoln as president, and the "house" began to fall. When he took office in March 1861, seven states had left the United States and formed the Confederate States of America. Within months, Virginia, Arkansas, North Carolina, and Tennessee would join them. Lincoln said he would fight to save the Union.

Rebels fired on Fort Sumter, a U.S. military base in South Carolina, on April 12, 1861. The Civil War that followed lasted four years and took the lives of more than 600,000 Americans.

Lincoln thought slavery was wrong, but he said it was legally protected in states where it already existed. When he became president, he promised not to interfere with states that had slaves. But when states began leaving the Union, Lincoln knew he had to confront the issue of slavery. In early 1863, he issued the Emancipation Proclamation, which said all enslaved people living in Confederate states were free. This act emboldened the slaves, who had already begun to desert their masters in droves. About 200,000 of these freedmen went north to fight in the war.

On April 9, 1865, Robert E. Lee, the Confederate general, surrendered at Appomattox Court House, Virginia, to U.S. General Ulysses S. Grant. The war was over and the Union had won.

Five days later, Lincoln and his wife, Mary, went to see a play. At Ford's Theatre, an actor named John Wilkes Booth shot the president. Lincoln died the next morning.

Lincoln visits troops in Antietam, Maryland, in October 1862.

## KEY DATES

**1861:** Civil War breaks out when Confederate troops fire on Fort Sumter, SC.

**1862:** Confederates defeated at Antietam, MD; Union army defeated at Fredericksburg, VA.

**1863:** Lincoln issues Emancipation Proclamation, freeing all slaves in areas of conflict.

**1863:** Union wins battle in Gettysburg, PA; Grant's Union troops win at Vicksburg, MS.

**1864:** Grant is made commander of all Union forces; Confederates abandon Atlanta. Lincoln is reelected to office.

**1865:** Union captures Richmond, VA; General Lee surrenders to Grant at Appomattox Court House, VA.

## Did You Know?

Nearly 500,000 soldiers died in the Civil War. That's about half of the total deaths of Americans in wars since the country began.

# Andrew Johnson ★

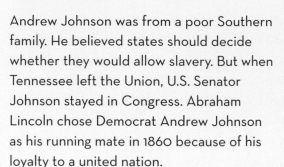

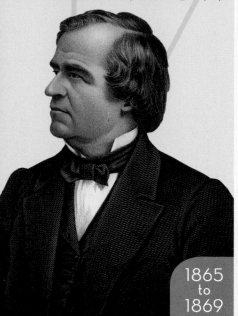

Andrew Johnson was from a poor Southern family. He believed states should decide whether they would allow slavery. But when Tennessee left the Union, U.S. Senator Johnson stayed in Congress. Abraham Lincoln chose Democrat Andrew Johnson as his running mate in 1860 because of his loyalty to a united nation.

On April 15, 1865, Lincoln died and Johnson became president. He needed to unify the North and South. He allowed southern states to pick their leaders and decide how to treat the newly freed African Americans.

Northern Republicans in Congress were angry. They wanted to limit former southern leaders' government involvement and eliminate southern laws that restricted the basic rights of formerly enslaved people.

Johnson did not want former slaves to become citizens, but in 1866, Congress passed the 14th Amendment, which gave citizenship to African Americans. It also set up military governments in the South to help with Reconstruction—rebuilding—after the war.

Johnson and Congress agreed on very little. In 1868, Congress impeached the president, charging him with breaking laws and abusing his powers. Congress held a trial to remove Johnson from office, but he was found not guilty and served out his term.

1865
to
1869

## 17TH PRESIDENT

**BORN:** December 29, 1808, in Raleigh, NC

**DIED:** July 31, 1875, in Carter County, TN

**POLITICAL PARTY:** Democratic

**VICE PRESIDENT:** None

**WIFE:** Eliza McCardle

**CHILDREN:** Martha, Charles, Mary, Robert, Andrew

## KEY DATES

**1865:** 13th Amendment to the Constitution is ratified, prohibiting slavery.

**1867:** The U.S. buys Alaska Territory from Russia.

**1869:** First railroad across continental U.S. is completed.

# Ulysses S. Grant

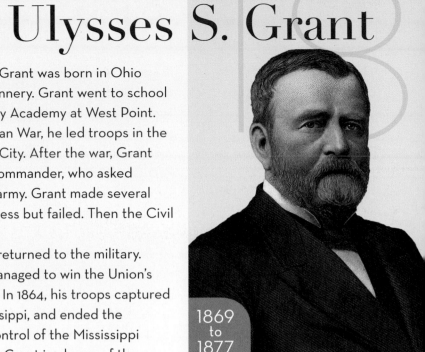

Ulysses Simpson Grant was born in Ohio and raised in a tannery. Grant went to school at the U.S. Military Academy at West Point. During the Mexican War, he led troops in the Battle of Mexico City. After the war, Grant argued with his commander, who asked him to leave the army. Grant made several attempts in business but failed. Then the Civil War began.

In 1861, Grant returned to the military. Grant's troops managed to win the Union's first major battle. In 1864, his troops captured Vicksburg, Mississippi, and ended the Confederacy's control of the Mississippi River. Lincoln put Grant in charge of the Union armies after this success. On April 9, 1865, General Grant accepted the surrender of Confederate General Robert E. Lee at Appomattox Court House, Virginia.

Grant won the presidential election in 1868 and again in 1872. But he wasn't a strong political leader. During his terms, dishonest deals were made by people in his government. Grant wasn't involved directly, but he did nothing to stop them. Because of the scandals, the Republican Party didn't select him to run for a third term.

1869 to 1877

Julia Grant

## 18TH PRESIDENT

**BORN:** April 27, 1822, in Point Pleasant, OH

**DIED:** July 23, 1885, in Mount McGregor, NY

**POLITICAL PARTY:** Republican

**VICE PRESIDENTS:** Schuyler Colfax, Henry Wilson

**WIFE:** Julia Boggs Dent

**CHILDREN:** Frederick, Ulysses, Ellen, Jesse

1872: Yellowstone becomes the first national park.

1876: Sitting Bull's Sioux defeat Lt. Col. Custer's troops in Montana.

# Rutherford B. Hayes

1877
to
1881

## 19TH PRESIDENT

**BORN:** October 4, 1822, in Delaware, OH

**DIED:** January 17, 1893, in Fremont, OH

**POLITICAL PARTY:** Republican

**VICE PRESIDENT:** William A. Wheeler

**WIFE:** Lucy Ware Webb

**CHILDREN:** Birchard Austin, James, Rutherford, Fanny, Scott Russell*

*Three other children died in infancy.

The presidency of Rutherford Birchard Hayes got off to a bumpy start. In his 1876 election against Samuel Tilden, the votes of three states were disputed. A U.S. government committee was formed to make a ruling. To win the votes of the disputed states, Hayes agreed to remove federal troops from the South and let southerners govern themselves. The deal pleased the committee. Hayes won the presidency—and got the nickname "Ruther*fraud*."

Hayes had fought for the United States in the Civil War. While on the battlefield, he was elected a U.S. representative from Ohio. Later he served two terms as governor before running for president.

Hayes felt his job as president was "to wipe out the color line." But when he ended Reconstruction, equal rights laws were soon broken.

Hayes wanted to regain the citizens' trust. He fought for equal education for African-American children in the South. And he worked to end the death penalty for criminals. He didn't run for a second term.

> "Nothing brings out the lower traits of human nature like office seeking."
> —Rutherford B. Hayes

## KEY DATES

**1877:** Reconstruction ends; federal troops leave the South. Tchaikovsky writes *Swan Lake*.

**1879:** Hayes decides not to run for a second term.

**1881:** The infamous frontier outlaw Billy the Kid dies in New Mexico.

# James Garfield

James Abram Garfield's father died when James was an infant. Born and raised in Ohio, he helped his mother on the farm and seldom went to school. But when he was older, he studied religion, went to college, and became a professor. Garfield was elected an Ohio state senator and then fought in the Civil War. In 1862, he led a battle in Kentucky that gave the Union control of half the state. Soon he became the youngest major general in the military.

After the war, Garfield served in the U.S. House of Representatives. He was on the committee that helped decide the 1876 presidential election.

As president, Garfield wanted to make the U.S. economy stronger. He wanted to put an end to the spoils system, which gave members of the winning political party government jobs even if they weren't qualified.

But tragedy struck. Charles J. Guiteau was angry because he wanted one of those government jobs. He shot President Garfield at a Washington , D.C., railroad station on July 2, 1881. Garfield lived for several weeks. He died on September 19, just six months after taking office.

March to September
**1881**

## 20TH PRESIDENT

**BORN:** November 19, 1831, in Moreland Hills, OH

**DIED:** September 19, 1881, in Elberon, NJ

**POLITICAL PARTY:** Republican

**VICE PRESIDENT:** Chester A. Arthur

**WIFE:** Lucretia Rudolph

**CHILDREN:** Harry, James R., Mary, Irvin, Abram*

*Two other children died in infancy.

Garfield's mother, who raised him alone, was the first mother of a president to attend an inauguration.

**1881:** Clara Barton establishes the American Red Cross.

**1881:** A school for African-American teachers, with Booker T. Washington as principal, opens.

# Chester A. Arthur

**1881 to 1885**

## 21ST PRESIDENT

**BORN:** October 5, 1829, in North Fairfield, VT

**DIED:** November 18, 1886, in New York, NY

**POLITICAL PARTY:** Republican

**VICE PRESIDENT:** None

**WIFE:** Ellen Herndon

**CHILDREN:** William, Chester II, Nellie

During the Civil War, Chester Allan Arthur was in charge of supplies for United States soldiers from New York. As a lawyer after the war, he worked to help African Americans receive fair treatment. His work made Arthur popular with some politicians.

Before he was president, Arthur benefited from the spoils system. Under President Grant, he received a job running the ports of New York since he was helpful to the Republican Party. Arthur then gave thousands of government jobs to other party members.

Arthur was picked to be vice president on James Garfield's ticket. When the newly elected president was killed, Arthur became president.

Like Garfield, Arthur worked to eliminate the spoils system. He supported a system that gave out government jobs based solely on a person's abilities. He also went after postal service employees who had accepted bribes in exchange for government contracts.

Arthur was a one-term president. He didn't seek reelection because he was very sick. He died of kidney failure in 1886. He is remembered as a president who was unexpectedly honest and hardworking.

> "Good ballplayers make good citizens."
> —Chester A. Arthur

## KEY DATES

**1882:** In an attempt to protect jobs, a 10-year ban begins on Chinese workers coming to the U.S.

**1884:** The population of the U.S. reaches 50 million.

**1885:** President Arthur dedicates the Washington Monument on the first president's birthday.

# Grover Cleveland

Grover Cleveland was the only president to serve two terms that were separated by another president's term. He was the 22nd and the 24th president.

Cleveland was born in New Jersey. His father died when he was 16 and so he could not go to college. He landed a job in a lawyer's office, where he learned the law. Cleveland started his political career as mayor of Buffalo, New York, and in 1882, he became governor of the state. In 1884, he was elected president.

Cleveland was the first Democrat in the White House in 26 years. He wanted to reduce tariffs, or taxes on foreign goods, and increase foreign trade. He tried to reform the tariff laws, but he failed. Congress wanted to protect U.S.-made goods.

Cleveland lost the election of 1888 to Benjamin Harrison. In 1892, he ran for president again and beat Harrison. The economy was in bad shape during his second term. In the Great Panic of 1893, many Americans lost their jobs and businesses. When railroad workers went on strike near Chicago, Illinois, Cleveland sent federal troops to restore order.

His actions against the workers, plus the long economic depression, lost Cleveland the support of the country.

1885-89
&
1893-97

## 22ND & 24TH PRESIDENT

**BORN:** March 18, 1837, in Caldwell, NJ

**DIED:** June 24, 1908, in Princeton, NJ

**POLITICAL PARTY:** Democratic

**VICE PRESIDENTS:** Thomas Hendricks, Adlai Stevenson

**WIFE:** Frances Folsom

**CHILDREN:** Ruth, Esther, Marion, Richard, Francis Grover

1886: Statue of Liberty is dedicated in New York Harbor.

1893: New Zealand becomes the first country in the world to give women the right to vote.

# Benjamin Harrison ★

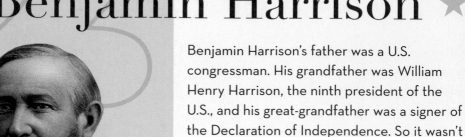

1889 to 1893

## 23RD PRESIDENT

**BORN:** August 20, 1833, in North Bend, OH

**DIED:** March 13, 1901, in Indianapolis, IN

**POLITICAL PARTY:** Republican

**VICE PRESIDENT:** Levi P. Morton

**WIVES:** Caroline Lavinia Scott, Mary Scott Lord

**CHILDREN:** Russell, Benjamin, Mary, Elizabeth

Benjamin Harrison's father was a U.S. congressman. His grandfather was William Henry Harrison, the ninth president of the U.S., and his great-grandfather was a signer of the Declaration of Independence. So it wasn't a surprise when Benjamin Harrison ended up in the White House.

Harrison was born in Ohio. He was a good student and studied law and practiced in Indiana. He served in the Civil War and became a U.S. senator from Indiana.

Harrison defeated President Grover Cleveland in the election of 1888. During his term, he raised tariffs on foreign goods to help U.S. businesses. Harrison and Congress also worked to pass the Sherman Antitrust Act in 1890. This law encouraged competition in the U.S. marketplace, allowing big and small companies many of the same advantages.

Harrison helped the United States gain respect from other nations. He made sure foreign nations sold U.S. goods. He led the very first Pan-American Conference, a meeting of the leaders of North, Central, and South America, and enacted a pension plan for Civil War veterans. But Americans had grown tired of government spending and higher prices on imported goods. Former President Cleveland ran against Harrison again in 1892. This time Cleveland won.

## KEY DATES

**1889:** Indian Territory is opened to white settlers. Eiffel Tower is completed in Paris, France.

**1890:** Last major battle of Indian Wars is fought at Wounded Knee in South Dakota.

**1892:** Ellis Island becomes main entry for foreigners coming to U.S.

# ★ William McKinley

During the Civil War, Rutherford B. Hayes wrote of one of his soldiers, "Every one admires [Captain McKinley] ... as one of the bravest and finest young officers of the army." He couldn't have known at the time that one future president was writing about another.

William McKinley impressed people because he was cheerful, wise, and respectful. He was born in Ohio and worked as a teacher before the Civil War. After, he studied law and went into politics. He was a U.S. congressman and then an Ohio governor.

In 1896, he ran as the Republican presidential candidate and won. When McKinley took office, Cuba was fighting for its independence from Spain. McKinley was eager to avoid the war. Then the U.S. battleship *Maine* blew up in the harbor of Havana, Cuba, and the Spanish were blamed. This was the beginning of the Spanish-American War, which lasted 100 days. The Treaty of Paris ended the war on April 11, 1899. It gave Cuba independence from Spain. The U.S. gained the territories of Puerto Rico, Guam, and the Philippine Islands.

McKinley won reelection in 1900. The next year, he was visiting the Pan-American Exposition, a world's fair in Buffalo, New York, when he was shot by an assassin. McKinley died eight days later.

## 1897 to 1901

## 25TH PRESIDENT

**BORN:** January 29, 1843, in Niles, OH

**DIED:** September 14, 1901, in Buffalo, NY

**POLITICAL PARTY:** Republican

**VICE PRESIDENTS:** Garret Hobart, Theodore Roosevelt

**WIFE:** Ida Saxton

**CHILDREN:** Katherine, Ida

**1897:** First subway, or underground train, in the U.S. opens in Boston, MA.

**1899:** U.S. troops go to China to help protect Europeans from a rebellion against foreigners.

# Teddy Roosevelt

1901 to 1909

## 26TH PRESIDENT

**BORN:** October 27, 1858, in New York, NY

**DIED:** January 6, 1919, in Oyster Bay, NY

**POLITICAL PARTY:** Republican; Bull-Moose

**VICE PRESIDENT:** Charles W. Fairbanks

**WIVES:** Alice Lee, Edith Kermit Carow

**CHILDREN:** Alice, Theodore, Kermit, Ethel, Archibald, Quentin

As a child, Theodore Roosevelt suffered from asthma. His father taught him to exercise and explore the outdoors.

> "Speak softly and carry a big stick."
> —Theodore Roosevelt

After graduating from Harvard, Roosevelt married, and was elected to the New York state legislature. In 1884, his wife, Alice, died, and Roosevelt moved to North Dakota, where he became a cattle rancher. Two years later, he returned to New York and remarried. He was head of New York City's police and then assistant secretary of the Navy.

In 1898, the Spanish-American War began. Roosevelt formed a volunteer army called the Rough Riders and became a war hero. Upon his return, he was easily elected governor of New York. Then, in 1900, he became vice president. When McKinley was assassinated, Roosevelt became president. The American people liked him, and in the 1904 election, Roosevelt won the presidency.

As president, Roosevelt used the powers of his office to force businesses to be fair to workers. He broke up strikes that hurt the nation's economy. And he took over the building of the Panama Canal. His most enduring legacy was setting aside wilderness lands so they would not be developed.

## KEY DATES

**1903:** Brothers Orville and Wilbur Wright make the first flight in a powered plane.

**1908:** Ford Motor Co. produces the Model T.

**1909:** Explorers Robert E. Peary and Matthew Henson reach the North Pole.

#  ★ ★ William H. Taft

William Howard Taft was an unlikely presidential candidate. He disliked running for office. He once said, "Politics, when I am in it, makes me sick."

Taft was born in Ohio. He studied at Yale University and then practiced law and became a judge. He wanted to be a justice on the U.S. Supreme Court. Taft's wife, Nellie, however, had a bigger dream. She wanted to be first lady.

Theodore Roosevelt and Taft admired each other's talents. When Roosevelt was president, he made Taft his secretary of war. And when Roosevelt decided not to run again in 1908, he asked his supporters to choose Taft. Nellie had to persuade Taft to accept the nomination.

Taft said the campaign was "one of the most uncomfortable four months of my life," but he won. As president, Taft disappointed Roosevelt. Taft worked to break up large businesses. Roosevelt felt Taft was being unfair. In 1912, Roosevelt ran against Taft. It split the Republican vote, and both men lost to the Democratic candidate.

After he left office, Taft taught law. In 1921, his dream came true. He was named chief justice of the United States by President Harding, becoming the only president to also serve on the Supreme Court.

1909 to 1913

## 27TH PRESIDENT

**BORN:** September 15, 1857, in Cincinnati, OH

**DIED:** March 8, 1930, in Washington, D.C.

**POLITICAL PARTY:** Republican

**VICE PRESIDENT:** James S. Sherman

**WIFE:** Helen (Nellie) Herron

**CHILDREN:** Robert Alphonso, Helen, Charles Phelps

**1910:** Boy Scouts of America is established.

**1912:** The *Titanic* sinks on its first voyage; more than 1,500 drown.

# 28 Woodrow Wilson

1913 to 1921

## 28TH PRESIDENT

**BORN:** December 28, 1856, in Staunton, VA

**DIED:** February 3, 1924, in Washington, D.C.

**POLITICAL PARTY:** Democratic

**VICE PRESIDENT:** Thomas R. Marshall

**WIVES:** Ellen Louise Axson, Edith Bolling Galt

**CHILDREN:** Margaret, Jessie, Eleanor

Thomas Woodrow Wilson was born in Virginia. His early memories were of a land torn by the Civil War.

> "If you want to make enemies, try to change something."
> —Woodrow Wilson

Wilson practiced law, became a professor and president of Princeton University, and governor of New Jersey.

As president, Wilson helped establish shorter workdays, pass child labor laws, and assist farmers with getting loans. But he worked against racial equality. Under his leadership, government offices were segregated for the first time since Reconstruction.

In 1917, the U.S. entered World War I, and a year later, an armistice was signed.

Wilson wanted to ensure fair terms of peace with a plan called the Fourteen Points. It called for an end to secret agreements between nations and for open trade. He fought to establish the League of Nations, an organization that would find peaceful solutions to conflicts. Sadly, the League failed.

In 1919, Wilson won the Nobel Peace Prize for his efforts to secure lasting peace. Shortly after, he suffered a stroke. Wilson was seldom seen in public for the remainder of his second term.

## KEY DATES

**1913:** Panama Canal is completed. Zippers become widely used in clothing.

**1917:** U.S. declares war on Germany and enters World War I.

**1920:** 19th Amendment to the Constitution gives women the right to vote.

# Warren G. Harding

Warren Gamaliel Harding was born in Ohio in 1865. He worked for a newspaper and studied law for a short time. He bought a small newspaper and made it successful. He became lieutenant governor of Ohio, a state senator, and then a U.S. senator.

Harding almost never spoke his mind and seldom cast a vote as senator. When the Republican Party couldn't agree on a 1920 presidential candidate, they selected Senator Harding as a compromise.

Harding believed the job of president was one with few responsibilities. He thought Congress should make America's decisions. Yet he appointed strong cabinet members, including Andrew Mellon, who shaped America's system of banking and taxes. But Harding thought government should support the rights of businesses rather than individuals. He made a point of not using his powers to help farmers or people without jobs.

Bribery scandals plagued Harding's time in office. The most famous was the Teapot Dome Scandal, in which a company was allowed to drill for oil on land set aside for the U.S. Navy.

In 1923, Harding and his wife, Flossie, took a trip out west. During their trip, Harding became ill. He died suddenly with his wife by his side. Flossie later destroyed many of Harding's personal papers to avoid more gossip.

1921
to
1923

## 29TH PRESIDENT

**BORN:** November 2, 1865, in Bloomington Grove, OH

**DIED:** August 2, 1923, in San Francisco, CA

**POLITICAL PARTY:** Republican

**VICE PRESIDENT:** Calvin Coolidge

**WIFE:** Florence "Flossie" Kling

**CHILDREN:** Elizabeth Ann Blaesing

**1921:** U.S. declares official end of war with Germany and Austria. U.S. population is 108 million.

**1922:** Louis Armstrong's trumpet playing takes Chicago by storm; jazz replaces ragtime as nation's music craze.

# Calvin Coolidge  ★ ★

John Calvin Coolidge was born in Vermont. He became a lawyer and a state senator in Massachusetts and then governor. Later he became Warren Harding's vice president. Coolidge's father, a notary public, swore him in as the new president when Harding died.

After Coolidge took office, news spread of the illegal deals of some of Harding's advisors. But Coolidge hadn't taken part in the deals. In 1924, Coolidge was elected to a second term.

In the 1920s, also known as the Roaring Twenties, many businesses were profitable and Americans invested in them heavily. African Americans found jobs in northern cities. And America was having a cultural renaissance in the arts. In 1924, Coolidge signed the Indian Citizenship Act, granting American Indians U.S. Citizenship.

But farmers struggled and rural businesses lost money. Coolidge believed government shouldn't get involved and didn't support labor unions. Coolidge also signed laws that lowered taxes for many people—but especially for the very wealthy. This created a large income gap between the poor and rich. Coolidge chose not to run again in 1928. He never gave a reason to the public but told his wife he thought the economy was going to collapse.

**1923 to 1929**

## 30TH PRESIDENT

**BORN:** July 4, 1872, in Plymouth Notch, VT

**DIED:** January 5, 1933, in Northampton, MA

**POLITICAL PARTY:** Republican

**VICE PRESIDENT:** Charles G. Dawes

**WIFE:** Grace Anna Goodhue

**CHILDREN:** John, Calvin Jr.

# KEY DATES

**1925:** Nellie Tayloe Ross of Wyoming becomes first woman elected governor.

**1927:** Charles Lindbergh makes first solo nonstop flight across the Atlantic. Babe Ruth sets season record with 60 home runs.

# Herbert Hoover

Herbert Clark Hoover was born in Iowa in 1874. Both his parents died when he was young, and his uncle in Oregon raised him. He studied engineering at Stanford University and became an expert on mines. Hoover traveled all over the world running mines and making his fortune.

When World War I began, Hoover helped organize efforts to let 120,000 Americans stranded in Europe return to the U.S. He also ran agencies in Belgium that gave food and clothing to millions of people. In Harding's administration, Hoover served as secretary of commerce. Hoover became known as a man who cared about others. When he ran for president, he won easily.

In his first year as president, the U.S. economy failed. Millions of people lost their jobs, and businesses and banks closed. This time became known as the Great Depression and was the country's worst economic crisis to date. Although the failed economy wasn't Hoover's fault, Americans blamed him for not reacting to it vigorously. Shantytowns filled with people who had lost their homes became known as "Hoovervilles."

Hoover ran for reelection in 1932, but with the nation still in deep trouble, people wanted a new approach to the crisis. Hoover lost to Franklin D. Roosevelt.

1929
to
1933

## 31ST PRESIDENT

**BORN:** August 10, 1874, in West Branch, IA

**DIED:** October 20, 1964, in New York, NY

**POLITICAL PARTY:** Republican

**VICE PRESIDENT:** Charles Curtis

**WIFE:** Lou Henry

**CHILDREN:** Herbert Jr., Allan

**1929:** The stock market crashes, causing panic for millions of investors and deflation of currency.

**1931:** "The Star-Spangled Banner" officially becomes the U.S. national anthem.

# Franklin D. Roosevelt

1933 to 1945

## 32ND PRESIDENT

**BORN:** January 30, 1882, in Hyde Park, NY

**DIED:** April 12, 1945, in Warm Springs, GA

**POLITICAL PARTY:** Democratic

**VICE PRESIDENTS:** John Garner, Henry Wallace, Harry S. Truman

**WIFE:** Anna Eleanor Roosevelt

**CHILDREN:** Anna Eleanor, James, Elliott, Franklin Jr., John*

*One other child died in infancy.

Eleanor Roosevelt

On a cold January day in 1933, Senator Jennings Randolph of West Virginia watched with thousands of people

> "The only thing we have to fear is fear itself."
> —Franklin D. Roosevelt

as Franklin Delano Roosevelt took the oath of office. "I was scared to death," said Randolph. "Everyone I knew had lost faith in the system of government. And then Roosevelt started to speak."

Roosevelt was from a wealthy New York family. Not sure what he wanted to do, he had become involved in politics. He loved that it was a way to help people who were less fortunate than he was.

Roosevelt had started his political career as a New York senator, and also served as assistant secretary of the Navy. In 1921, he contracted polio, leaving him unable to walk. Roosevelt wasn't sure he'd ever run for office again, but he kept working for the Democrats. In 1928, he became the New York governor.

Four years later, he was elected president. Roosevelt motivated a nation that was suffering from the Great Depression. Millions of people had lost their jobs and were homeless. Roosevelt wanted people to know that the bad times wouldn't last forever.

As president of a struggling country, Roosevelt set up government agencies that created jobs, and pushed for laws that regulated fair pay. He established Social Security and insurance for the unemployed. He raised taxes on the wealthy to pay for these programs, which he called, collectively, the New Deal.

Many thought Roosevelt went too far. They said the government shouldn't get involved in business practices. But the voters were grateful for Roosevelt's programs. They reelected him in 1936 and again in 1940 and 1944!

When World War II began in Europe, Roosevelt believed the U.S. should go to the aid of the British. But most Americans felt the U.S. should stay out of the war. In 1941, German U-boats attacked American ships. And then Japan attacked Pearl Harbor in Hawaii on December 7, 1941. The next day, Congress declared war on Japan, making Roosevelt a wartime president.

For 42 months, U.S. troops fought with allies from Britain and the Soviet Union in battles in Europe, Africa, and Asia. Roosevelt worked with Britain's leader, Winston Churchill, and the Soviet leader, Joseph Stalin, to bring the war to an end. But he did not live to see the peace. He died in April 1945, three months into his fourth term in office. The war in Europe ended the next month, and Japan surrendered in September.

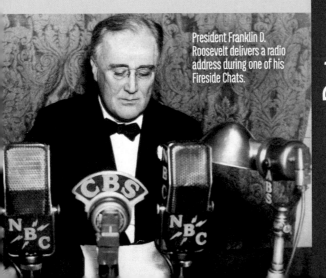

President Franklin D. Roosevelt delivers a radio address during one of his Fireside Chats.

## KEY DATES

**1934:** Severe drought hits central and southern plains states; Dust Bowl destroys farms.

**1936:** African-American runner Jesse Owens wins four gold medals at Olympics in Berlin, Germany. War breaks out between China and Japan.

**1938:** Germany annexes Austria. Anti-Jewish laws are passed in Italy. Howard Hughes flies around the world in three days and 19 hours.

**1939:** England and France declare war on Germany. *The Wizard of Oz* is released in U.S.

**1941:** U.S. declares war on Germany, Italy, and Japan; joins Allies in World War II.

**1944:** Allied troops invade Normandy, France in D-day, battle to defeat the Nazis.

## Did You Know?

ROOSEVELT

FDR was the only president to be elected to more than two terms in office. In 1951, the 22nd Amendment to the Constitution set a limit of two terms.

49

# Harry S. Truman

1945
to
1953

## 33RD PRESIDENT

**BORN:** May 8, 1884, in Lamar, MO

**DIED:** December 26, 1972, in Kansas City, MO

**POLITICAL PARTY:** Democratic

**VICE PRESIDENT:** Alben W. Barkley

**WIFE:** Elizabeth (Bess) Virginia Wallace

**CHILDREN:** Margaret

Margaret and Bess Truman

Harry S. Truman was born and raised in Missouri. His family struggled financially, so instead of going to college, he ran the family farm. After fighting in World War I, Truman became a county court judge.

> "America was not built on fear. America was built on courage, on imagination and an unbeatable determination to do the job at hand."
> —Harry S. Truman

Then he was elected a U.S. senator. He joined President Roosevelt's ticket in his last term and was elected vice president. Truman had been vice president for only 82 days when President Roosevelt died. Suddenly, Truman was president.

World War II wasn't over yet. Japan was still fighting in the Pacific. Truman ordered the use of the atomic bomb against Japan. The U.S. bombed two cities—Nagasaki and Hiroshima—killing as many as 200,000 civilians. The Japanese surrendered.

At home, Truman tried to continue Roosevelt's policies with the Fair Deal. Truman believed the government should help Americans find work in fair conditions without discrimination. He also supported the GI Bill, which paid for returning soldiers to go to college.

After World War II, the Soviet Union wanted to expand its control of Eastern Europe and its form of government, called communism. The U.S. tried to keep this from happening. The resulting tensions, known as the Cold War, would shape American politics for decades.

★ ★ ★ ★

In 1950, the Korean War began. Truman sent U.S. troops to assist South Korea while China supported North Korea. The war ended in 1953, and Korea remained divided.

**Atomic bombs dropped on Nagasaki and Hiroshima in 1945 led to a quick surrender by Japan.**

The *Enola Gay*, a Boeing B-29, became the first aircraft to drop an atomic bomb, on August 6, 1945.

# KEY DATES

**1945:** United Nations is established. Germany and Japan surrender, and World War II ends.

**1946:** Robert E. Byrd begins his expedition to the South Pole.

**1947:** *The Diary of Anne Frank* is published. Jackie Robinson becomes the first black player to join Major League Baseball.

**1949:** Indonesia gains independence from the Netherlands; Vietnam from France.

**1950:** North Korean troops attack South Korea. 1.5 million TV sets are in use in the U.S.

**1951:** The 22nd Amendment to the Constitution limits the U.S. president to two terms in office.

## Did You Know?

Truman didn't have a middle name, only the initial *S*. His parents used the initial to honor their fathers, who had names that began with *S*.

# Dwight D. Eisenhower

**I LIKE IKE**

People liked Ike, as young Dwight David Eisenhower was called growing up. After he was born in Texas, Eisenhower's family moved to Kansas and settled on a farm. Ike knew early on he wanted a career in the army, so he went to the U.S. Military Academy at West Point, in New York.

During World War II, Eisenhower was in charge of all Allied troops in Europe. By the end of the war, he was the highest-ranked soldier in the U.S. military. He returned home a hero in 1945.

Eisenhower had the opportunity to run for president as a Democrat in 1948, but he passed up the chance. In 1952, he ran as a Republican and won easily.

As president, Eisenhower helped end the Korean War. He also tried to ease tensions between the Soviet Union and the U.S.

At home, black Americans were still being treated unfairly. In 1954, the Supreme Court ruled in *Brown v. Board of Education of Topeka* that separating children into schools by race was illegal. Eisenhower didn't like the ruling, but he still sent troops to escort students into school in Little Rock, Arkansas, in 1957. When he left office, more than 90 percent of African-American children still attended separate schools.

1953 to 1961

## 34TH PRESIDENT

**BORN:** October 14, 1890, in Denison, TX

**DIED:** March 28, 1969, in Washington, D.C.

**POLITICAL PARTY:** Republican

**VICE PRESIDENT:** Richard M. Nixon

**WIFE:** Marie (Mamie) Geneva Doud

**CHILDREN:** Doud Dwight, John Sheldon

## KEY DATES

**1955:** Rosa Parks is arrested after refusing to give up her bus seat to a white man.

**1956:** Minimum wage for workers is raised from 75 cents to $1.00 per hour.

**1959:** Hawaii becomes 50th state. More than 85 million TV sets are in use in the U.S.

# John F. Kennedy

★

John Fitzgerald Kennedy came from a large, politically active Massachusetts family. When the U.S. entered World War II, Kennedy joined the navy. After the war, Kennedy was elected to the U.S. House of Representatives and then to the U.S. Senate. In 1960, Kennedy ran for president against Vice President Richard Nixon. Their debates were the first ever shown on television. Kennedy looked young and smart while Nixon appeared old and unprepared. Kennedy won in a close election.

In October 1962, Soviet missiles were stationed in Cuba, only 90 miles from Florida. Kennedy told the Soviet Union (Russia today) to remove them or face U.S. force. After 13 days, the Soviet Union backed down.

Kennedy proposed laws to give African Americans equal rights. He created the Peace Corps to send Americans to aid people abroad and share cultural understanding between nations. He also worked to push the U.S. space program forward.

On November 22, 1963, Kennedy was shot while riding in a motorcade in Texas. He died at the hospital.

> "Ask not what your country can do for you; ask what you can do for your country."
> —John F. Kennedy

1961 to 1963

## 35TH PRESIDENT

**BORN:** May 29, 1917, in Brookline, MA

**DIED:** November 22, 1963, in Dallas, TX

**POLITICAL PARTY:** Democratic

**VICE PRESIDENT:** Lyndon B. Johnson

**WIFE:** Jacqueline Lee Bouvier

**CHILDREN:** Caroline, John*

*One other child died in infancy.

**1962:** First lady gives tour of White House on TV; eight out of 10 TVs are tuned in.

**1963:** Martin Luther King, Jr. delivers, "I Have a Dream" speech at March on Washington.

# Lyndon B. Johnson ★

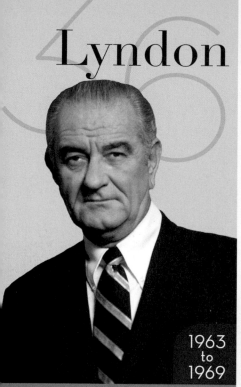

**1963 to 1969**

## 36TH PRESIDENT

**BORN:** August 27, 1908, near Stonewall, TX

**DIED:** January 22, 1973, in San Antonio, TX

**POLITICAL PARTY:** Democratic

**VICE PRESIDENT:** Hubert H. Humphrey

**WIFE:** Claudia Alta (Lady Bird) Taylor

**CHILDREN:** Lynda Bird, Luci Baines

Fewer than two hours after President Kennedy was killed, Vice President Lyndon Baines Johnson was sworn in as president.

Johnson had entered politics hoping to improve Americans' lives. A former Senate majority leader, he had good relationships in Congress. He used these to pass the Civil Rights Act and the Voting Rights Act. He began Head Start, an early education program. And he worked to pass Medicare and Medicaid plans to provide free health care to the elderly and poor. Johnson easily won the 1964 election.

In office, he launched a program called the "Great Society," which was designed to fight social and racial inequality. But his presidency was overshadowed by the Vietnam War. U.S. troops had been in Vietnam for nearly ten years. Johnson sent hundreds of thousands of drafted American soldiers into the fight. Protests against the draft and the war were staged across the country.

Johnson no longer wanted to be the leader of a divided nation. At the end of his first full term, he announced that he would not run for another. He retired to his ranch in Texas.

> "If government is to serve any purpose, it is to do for others what they are unable to do for themselves."
>
> —Lyndon B. Johnson

## KEY DATES

**1964:** Congress passes Civil Rights Act banning discrimination. The Beatles arrive in America.

**1967:** First successful human heart transplant takes place.

**1968:** Martin Luther King, Jr. is killed; U.S. Senator Robert Kennedy is shot two months later.

# ★ Richard M. Nixon

Richard Milhous Nixon was born in California. He became a lawyer and served in the navy during World War II. After the war, he was elected to Congress. During the 1950s,

> "I like the job I have, but if I had to live my life over again, I would like to have ended up a sportswriter."
>
> —Richard M. Nixon

Nixon made a name for himself by leading an investigation looking for communist spies in the U.S. government. In 1953, he became Dwight D. Eisenhower's vice president.

Nixon lost the 1960 election to John F. Kennedy. He ran again in 1968 and won. He was reelected in 1972. Nixon had a remarkable presidency. For many years, the U.S., China, and the Soviet Union had been enemies. Nixon visited China and the Soviet Union and set the stage for better relations. During Nixon's second term, U.S. involvement in the Vietnam War ended.

In 1972, five men working for the committee to reelect Nixon were arrested after breaking into the Democratic Party offices in a building called Watergate. Nixon lied to cover up the break-in. He resigned in disgrace before he could be impeached by Congress.

He was the first and only president to resign. Many Americans felt he had betrayed them.

1969 to 1974

## 37TH PRESIDENT

**BORN:** January 9, 1913, in Yorba Linda, CA

**DIED:** April 22, 1994, in New York, NY

**POLITICAL PARTY:** Republican

**VICE PRESIDENTS:** Spiro T. Agnew, Gerald R. Ford

**WIFE:** Thelma Catherine (Pat) Ryan

**CHILDREN:** Patricia, Julie

**1969:** *Apollo II* astronaut Neil Armstrong becomes the first person to walk on the moon.

**1973:** Vice President Spiro Agnew resigns office, accused of breaking laws while governor of Maryland.

# Gerald R. Ford

1974
to
1977

## 38TH PRESIDENT

**BORN:** July 14, 1913, in Omaha, NE

**DIED:** December 26, 2006, in Rancho Mirage, CA

**POLITICAL PARTY:** Republican

**VICE PRESIDENT:** Nelson A. Rockefeller

**WIFE:** Elizabeth (Betty) Anne Bloomer

**CHILDREN:** Michael, John, Steven, Susan

Millions of Americans watched President Nixon on television the night he resigned, including Vice President Gerald Rudolph Ford and his family.

Ford was born in Nebraska and raised in Michigan. He was a good student. He was a star football player at the University of Michigan. Ford went to Yale Law School before serving in the navy during World War II.

In 1948, Ford was elected a U.S. representative from Michigan and stayed in that position for 25 years. President Nixon asked him to become vice president in 1973 when Spiro Agnew resigned. A year later, Ford became the only person to hold the office of president without being chosen by the voters for president or vice president.

Ford pardoned Nixon, excusing him from any crimes he might have committed during his presidency. This made many people angry, but Ford felt the country should move on.

He had many other problems to handle. The U.S. economy was in its worst decline since the Great Depression, and the Cold War with the Soviet Union was heating up over nuclear missiles. Ford ran in the presidential election of 1976, hoping to win the office on his own, but he lost. Ford is most often remembered for ending the Nixon years' troubles.

## KEY DATES

**1975:** The Vietnam War ends as North Vietnamese troops overrun Siagon.

**1976:** U.S. celebrates its bicentennial—200th birthday—with events across the country.

# Jimmy Carter

James Earl Carter, Jr., always used the nickname "Jimmy." Raised on his family's peanut farm in Georgia, he grew up to be deeply religious. He studied nuclear physics at the United States Naval Academy and served as a submarine commander. Carter was a state senator and governor of Georgia before being elected president in 1976.

Carter believed in efficient government, ending unfair treatment of African Americans, and taking care of the environment.

But as president, Carter faced many problems. American energy use was increasing, and Middle Eastern nations raised oil prices dramatically. A shortage of gasoline created long lines at fuel pumps across America. Carter worked with Congress to pass the National Energy Act of 1978 to help make gas available and affordable. But voters were still unhappy.

In 1979, religious extremists took 52 Americans hostage at the U.S. embassy in Iran. Although the Carter administration's negotiations for the hostages' release were close to success, the crisis contributed to low approval ratings for Carter. He wasn't reelected in 1980, but he did not slow down. In 2002, Carter won the Nobel Peace Prize for his efforts to find peaceful solutions and promote human rights.

1977
to
1981

## 39TH PRESIDENT

**BORN:** October 1, 1923, in Plains, GA

**POLITICAL PARTY:** Democratic

**VICE PRESIDENT:** Walter F. Mondale

**WIFE:** Eleanor Rosalynn Smith

**CHILDREN:** John William, James Earl III, Jeffrey, Amy Lynn

**1977:** Carter forms the Department of Energy in response to a widespread energy crisis in the U.S.

**1978:** Israel and Egypt sign a peace agreement at Camp David in the U.S.

**1980:** The U.S. boycotts the Moscow Olympics to protest the war in Afghanistan.

# Ronald W. Reagan

1981
to
1989

## 40TH PRESIDENT

**BORN:** February 6, 1911, in Tampico, IL

**DIED:** June 5, 2004, in Bel-Air, CA

**POLITICAL PARTY:** Republican

**VICE PRESIDENT:** George H. W. Bush

**WIVES:** Jane Wyman, Nancy Davis

**CHILDREN:** Maureen, Michael, Patti, Ronald Jr.*

*One other child died in infancy.

Nancy Reagan

Ronald Wilson Reagan was well known to U.S. voters before he ever decided to run for office. He had been a movie and TV actor since the 1930s.

> "America is too great for small dreams."
> —Ronald W. Reagan

Reagan was born in Illinois; his family lived over the store where his father worked. Dutch, as he was nicknamed, loved sports and acting. After college, he got a job as a radio sports announcer. During World War II, he made training films for the Army.

In 1966, Reagan was elected governor of California and held that office until 1975. Because of his acting background, Reagan was comfortable in front of a camera. Voters liked his relaxed, confident style and, in 1980, elected him president.

Reagan's presidency began with exciting news from Iran. On the day Reagan took office, the Americans who had been held hostage for more than a year were freed. President Carter's aides had worked out their release before he left office. But the event set a positive tone for Reagan's first term.

Reagan thought that if the rich spent more money, it would "trickle down" and help all levels of the economy, so he lowered taxes for the wealthy. While much of the 1980s was a prosperous time for America, the failure of some banks and a massive increase in the national debt from government borrowing were marks against Reagan's legacy.

The Cold War leaders of the U.S. and the Soviet Union engaged in an arms race, which

increased spending on weapons. Then, in his second term, Reagan met with the leader of the Soviet Union, and their friendly talks led to a treaty in 1987 that reduced the supply of nuclear missiles.

When Reagan left office, many people felt he had made the world a safer place. He and the first lady, Nancy, retired to California. Reagan died in 2004 after a long illness.

Ronald Reagan addresses the people of West Berlin on June 12, 1987, at the base of the Brandenburg Gate, near the Berlin Wall. "Mr. Gorbachev, tear down this wall!" was his famous command to Soviet leader Mikhail Gorbachev.

## KEY DATES

**1981:** Astronauts John Young and Bob Crippen make the first test flight of a space shuttle, *Columbia*, the world's first reusable spacecraft.

**1984:** Soviet Union keeps its athletes out of the Summer Olympics in Los Angeles.

**1986:** Space shuttle *Challenger* explodes after liftoff, killing all seven crew members. It is televised as it happens.

**1987:** Joint congressional hearings on the Iran-Contra affair are on TV.

### Did You Know?

Reagan was the only president to survive an attempted assassination.

# George H. W. Bush

41

1989 to 1993

## 41ST PRESIDENT

**BORN:** June 12, 1924, in Milton, MA

**POLITICAL PARTY:** Republican

**VICE PRESIDENT:** J. Danforth (Dan) Quayle

**WIFE:** Barbara Pierce

**CHILDREN:** George Walker, Robin, John Ellis, Neil, Marvin, Dorothy

George and Barbara Bush

In an interview in *TIME* magazine one hundred days into his presidency, George Herbert Walker Bush said, "I do hope that history will say we helped make things a little kinder and gentler."

Bush was born to a wealthy New England family. He joined the navy during World War II as its youngest pilot. After the war, Bush married, went to college, and moved to Texas to work in the oil business.

His father had been a U.S. senator from Connecticut, and Bush wanted to enter politics. He was elected in Texas to the U.S. House of Representatives. Eventually, Bush served as the U.S. representative to the United Nations and China and as director of the Central Intelligence Agency. He then served as Ronald Reagan's vice president for two terms. In 1988, he was elected president.

In 1991, Iraq invaded Kuwait. This threatened U.S. interests in the Middle East, so Bush sent U.S. soldiers to fight in an action called Operation Desert Storm.

At home, the U.S. economy was in a recession. Despite promising no new taxes, President Bush was forced to raise them to keep the government running. Voters were unhappy with this, and Bush was not reelected in 1992. He moved to Houston, Texas, where he still lives today.

## KEY DATES

**1989:** Hundreds are killed rallying for democracy in Tiananmen Square. The Berlin Wall is torn down.

**1990:** South Africa frees Nelson Mandela. Germany is reunited. World Wide Web launches.

**1991:** The U.S.S.R. collapses, ending the Cold War.

# ★ ★ ★ Bill Clinton

William Jefferson Clinton was born in Hope, Arkansas. He went to college at Georgetown University and studied in England. At Yale Law School, he met Hillary Rodham, whom he would later marry.

A law career in Arkansas led to politics, and in 1978, Clinton became governor of Arkansas. In 1992, he ran as the Democratic presidential candidate.

Clinton improved the sluggish economy with a budget plan that increased taxes on the wealthy, cut government spending, and provided tax cuts to technology companies to encourage growth. For the first time in 30 years, the U.S. federal budget had a surplus.

Clinton's charisma and quick grasp of issues made him an able diplomat. He brokered talks between Middle East leaders and worked with Russia's Boris Yeltsin to bring an end to fighting in the former Yugoslavia.

Clinton was elected to a second term in 1996. During both of his terms, he faced charges of illegal behavior but was never found guilty. In late 1999, he was impeached. A trial in the U.S. Senate cleared him of all charges.

Clinton left the White House a very popular president. He continues to remain active in politics and in humanitarian causes through the Clinton Foundation.

1993 to 2001

## 42ND PRESIDENT

**BORN:** August 19, 1946, in Hope, AR

**POLITICAL PARTY:** Democratic

**VICE PRESIDENT:** Albert Gore, Jr.

**WIFE:** Hillary Rodham

**CHILDREN:** Chelsea

Chelsea, Hillary, and Bill Clinton

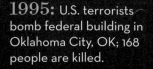

**1995:** U.S. terrorists bomb federal building in Oklahoma City, OK; 168 people are killed.

**2000:** First Lady Hillary Clinton is elected to U.S. Senate from New York.

# 43 George W. Bush ★ ★

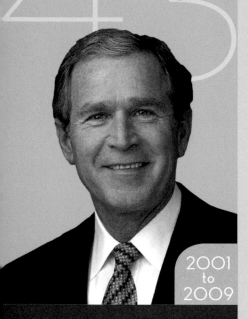

2001
to
2009

## 43RD PRESIDENT

**BORN:** July 6, 1946, in New Haven, CT

**POLITICAL PARTY:** Republican

**VICE PRESIDENT:** Richard Cheney

**WIFE:** Laura Welch

**CHILDREN:** Barbara, Jenna

The 2000 election between Vice President Al Gore, a Democrat, and Republican George Walker Bush was unusual. It came down to the votes in

> "We will not tire, we will not falter, and we will not fail."
> —George W. Bush

Florida, where the election was so close that the ballots had to be recounted several times. Finally, the U.S. Supreme Court declared Bush to be the winner. It was the first time an election was decided by the Supreme Court.

Bush came from a political family. His grandfather Prescott Bush had been a U.S. senator from Connecticut. His father, George, had been the 41st president, and his brother Jeb was the governor of Florida. Bush went to Yale and Harvard and then entered the oil business in Texas. In 1994, he was elected governor of Texas. Six years later, he became president.

Given the budget surplus from the Clinton years, Congress agreed to Bush's plan to lower taxes. President Bush signed the No Child Left Behind Act, which rewarded schools that raised students' test scores and penalized schools that did not.

Bush's biggest challenge in office began on September 11, 2001. Al-Qaeda terrorists led by Osama bin Laden hijacked airplanes and flew two of them into the World Trade Center towers in New York City. Another plane struck

A former teacher, First Lady Laura Bush championed education and literacy during her time in the White House.

the Pentagon near Washington, D.C., and a fourth crashed into a field in Pennsylvania. Less than a month after the attacks, Bush ordered U.S. troops to Afghanistan.

In 2003, Bush ordered the invasion of Iraq. He said that Iraqi president Saddam Hussein was a threat to the United States.

During Bush's second term, he dealt with the fallout from his administration's slow, bungled response to Hurricane Katrina, which slammed into the coasts of Louisiana and Mississippi in late August 2005.

President George W. Bush, standing next to retired firefighter Bob Beckwith, 68, speaks to volunteers and firefighters as he surveys the damage at the site of the World Trade Center in New York, September 2001.

# KEY DATES

**2001:** The worst terrorist attacks ever on U.S. soil occur.

**2002:** Fox reality TV show *American Idol* debuts. More than half the U.S. population uses the Internet regularly.

**2003:** Space shuttle *Columbia* explodes, killing all seven astronauts aboard.

**2004:** Bush is reelected. A powerful earthquake near Indonesia causes a tsunami killing more than 170,000 people in Asia and East Africa.

**2007:** Apple debuts the first version of the iPhone, changing personal communication.

## Did You Know?

Bush named the first African-American secretaries of state: Colin Powell and Condoleezza Rice

Condoleezza Rice

# Barack Obama

2009
to
2017

## 44TH PRESIDENT

**BORN:** August 4, 1961, in Honolulu, HI

**POLITICAL PARTY:** Democratic

**VICE PRESIDENT:** Joseph Biden

**WIFE:** Michelle LaVaughn Robinson

**CHILDREN:** Malia, Sasha

Malia, Michelle, Barack, and Sasha Obama with their pets Bo and Sunny

Barack Obama was born in Hawaii to a Kenyan father and an American mother. His parents divorced when he was a toddler, and

> "We are and always will be a nation of immigrants. We were strangers once, too."
> —Barack Obama

he lived for four years as a child in Indonesia before returning to Hawaii. He credits these experiences with broadening his worldview beyond his middle-class upbringing. After attending Columbia University in New York City, Obama moved to Chicago and worked as a community organizer, starting job training programs and a tenants' rights organization. He left Chicago for law school at Harvard in 1988. Upon earning his law degree, Obama returned to Chicago and worked at a law firm, where he met Michelle Robinson. Barack and Michelle married in 1992.

Obama went on to teach law school but remained active in the community and began a political career by serving three terms in the Illinois state senate. Following a loss in a run for a seat in the House of Representatives, he successfully ran for the U.S. Senate in 2004, earning the national spotlight. He was elected president in 2008.

Barack Obama was the first African-American president. When he took office in 2009, he inherited a nation facing a grave financial crisis and fighting wars in two countries. Obama began his first term with a promise to cut the country's war budget and bring U.S. soldiers home from Iraq and Afghanistan. By 2011, the U.S. military presence in Iraq was ended. Then, on May 1,

2011, President Obama announced to the world that Osama bin Laden, the man behind the September 11, 2001, terrorist attacks, had been located and killed in Pakistan.

Turning his attention to domestic matters, Obama aimed to unite Americans around policies to strengthen the economy, overhaul health care, and curb industrial impact on the environment. President Obama's most enduring legacy will most likely be the Patient Protection and Affordable Care Act—often referred to as "Obamacare." With this bill, passed in March 2010, health-care coverage became available to all citizens.

Some Americans opposed Obamacare, and they voiced their opinions during the midterm election in 2011. Republicans regained control in the House of Representatives when Democrats lost 63 of 435 seats. This change in power made it hard for Obama to pass other bills through Congress. As a result, he signed more executive actions than any other president— more than 230 in eight years.

# KEY DATES

**2009:** Obama is awarded the Nobel Peace Prize.

**2010:** A deepwater oil well in the Gulf of Mexico explodes, causing the worst environmental disaster in US history. It takes 86 days to repair the leaking well.

**2011:** Occupy Wall Street movement begins.

**2012:** Hurricane Sandy hits the northeastern United States and causes $75 billion in damage.

**2013:** Pope Francis of Argentina is elected as the first pope from the Americas.

**2015:** Same-sex marriage is legalized in all 50 U.S. states in a landmark decision by the Supreme Court.

**2015:** Cuba and the United States reestablish full diplomatic relations after 54 years of hostility.

## Did You Know?

Barack Obama won two Grammy Awards: one for Best Spoken Word Album for his reading of *Dreams From My Father*, his autobiography, and the other for the reading of his second book, *The Audacity of Hope*.

# Donald J. Trump ★ ★

Inaugurated
2017

## 45TH PRESIDENT

**BORN:** June 14, 1946

**POLITICAL PARTY:** Republican

**VICE PRESIDENT:** Mike Pence

**WIVES:** Ivana Marie Trump, Marla Maples, and Melania Trump

**CHILDREN:** Ivanka, Donald Jr., Eric, Tiffany, and Barron

Donald John Trump was born in New York City on June 14, 1946. As a teenager, Trump attended New York Military Academy, where he was an athlete and a student leader. He went to Fordham University and received a degree from the University of Pennsylvania. In 1968, he went to work for his father as a real-estate developer.

In 1971, Trump renamed his family business the Trump Organization. One of his first projects was a hotel in New York City. He renovated a building and relaunched the property in 1980 as the Grand Hyatt. The hotel was a success.

Two years later, Trump opened Trump Tower, a luxury skyscraper and tourist attraction in New York City. He continued to build his real-estate empire with casinos, resorts, and golf courses. He also ventured into new businesses, introducing Trump Steaks, Trump Natural Spring Water, and an airline called Trump Shuttle.

By the late 1990s, Trump's attention had turned to politics. He announced in 1999 that he would run for president. In order to enter the race, he changed his party affiliation from Republican to Reform Party. But he

Donald Jr., Melania, Donald, Ivanka, Eric and Tiffany Trump.

quit the campaign before the first primaries. Five years later, he was on TV, starring in the reality-television program *The Apprentice*. Although his show was a hit, Trump faced challenges in other parts of his life. In 2005, for-profit Trump University was sued by the state of New York. Four years later, his casino company filed for bankruptcy.

In 2015, in an event at Trump Tower, Trump announced again that he would run for president. Republican Party leaders at first dismissed his candidacy, but a groundswell of support from voters who were frustrated by the status quo carried him to a primary victory over a crowded field of Republican hopefuls. In July 2016, Trump accepted the nomination at the Republican National Convention in Cleveland, Ohio.

During the campaign, Trump faced scandals and criticism. He made controversial remarks about several groups of people, including Latinos, Muslims, African Americans, and women. This led many, including some Republican officials, to back away from him. Democrats also criticized his failure to release his tax returns. But Trump continued to receive wide support and thousands of people attended his rallies.

Trump's victory surprised many experts who had predicted his opponent, Democrat Hillary Clinton, would win. An election-night upset gave Trump a majority of votes in the electoral college. He would enter the White House with a Republican majority in both the Senate and House of Representatives, giving him ample support for his agenda.

## KEY DATES

**2015:** Donald J. Trump announces his candidacy for president.

**2016:** The Republican National Convention begins in Cleveland, OH.

**2016:** On November 8, 2016, Trump is elected president in a close race against Hillary Clinton.

**2017:** January 20th is Inauguration Day for the 45th president.

Republican president-elect Donald Trump delivers his acceptance speech in the early morning hours of November 9, 2016.

### Did You Know?

Donald Trump is the first person elected to the presidency without experience in either the government or the military.

# The Road to the White House

START

## ARE YOU READY TO RUN?

You'll need to meet a few requirements before you can run for president. According to the Constitution, you must be at least 35 years old and have lived in the United States for at least 14 years. You also must be a "natural-born" citizen. That means you must have been born as a citizen of the United States.

## RACE THROUGH THE PRIMARIES.

Before the main election, you must first persuade your party to nominate you. That means you have to beat other candidates in primaries or caucuses. These are elections in which the people of individual states decide who would be the best candidate on the Republican, Democratic, or Independent ticket. Most states run *primaries*, elections in which voters can secretly cast ballots for the candidate they would like to run. Ten states *caucus*. They hold meetings in which registered voters for a party gather to debate and decide who they want as a candidate.

## RAISE MONEY!

You'll need money to run your campaign. Once you have raised or spent $5,000, you must register with the Federal Election Commission (FEC).

## WHAT ARE DELEGATES?

Your performance in the primary elections or caucus determines how many delegates from each state will be sent to the nominating convention to vote for you. Each state sends a different number of delegates to the convention, based mostly on how many voters live in the state. In the Democratic Party, if you win 40% of the primary vote, 40% of the delegates sent by the state will represent you. But look out—delegates are allowed to vote however they want at the convention, regardless of who they have supported earlier! In the Republican Party, the rules are different depending on which state is sending the delegates. Some states send all their delegates in support of one candidate. Others split the delegates according to the number of votes won by each candidate.

## CONVENE!

Each party holds a *nominating convention* to determine who will be their candidate for president. Usually, the party knows who they will nominate before the convention, and a quick vote determines the candidate. But if the race is close, there may be several votes before the candidate is determined. This is called a *brokered convention*. In 1924, the Democratic National Convention voted 103 times before they agreed on a candidate! If your party nominates you, you are ready to run.

Check out the 2016 Conventions on the next page!

## CAMPAIGN!

As a presidential candidate, you will travel around the United States making speeches, giving interviews, and debating your opponent. Your goal is to persuade as many voters as possible to vote for you on Election Day. Try to run a fair campaign—that means you should talk about important issues, be honest about your plans, and try to avoid saying mean things about your opponent. You will campaign nonstop until Election Day, the Tuesday following the first Monday in November.

## CROSS YOUR FINGERS . . .

On Election Day, voters across the country will go to the polls to vote for their favorite candidate. (Voters must be at least 18 years old, be a citizen in good standing, and be registered to vote in their state.) If you can clinch the most *electoral votes*, you're the winner!

## TAKE THE OATH.

On January 20, you will be officially sworn in as president of the United States. Congratulations! You've just finished the longest, hardest race of your life. As president, you will earn a $400,000 salary.

## WHAT IS THE ELECTORAL COLLEGE?

Each state has a number of electoral votes based on how many people live in it. States with bigger populations get more votes. In most states, the candidate who wins the most votes from citizens gets all of the electoral votes. In the December after the election, the electors hold a meeting to register their states' votes. The candidate with the most electoral votes wins the election.

# 2016 Election Spotlight

## REPUBLICAN CONVENTION
### July 18–21, 2016 ★ Cleveland, OH

**Republican Nominee:** Donald Trump

**Fame Factor:** Experienced businessman

**Running Mate:** Mike Pence

**Fame Factor:** Governor of Indiana

**Convention Theme:** Make America Great Again

**Platforms:** Immigration reform, maintain law and order

"In this race to the White House . . . I am with you, I will fight for you, and I will win for you."

—Donald Trump's nomination acceptance speech

## INSIDE THE CONVENTION

Kid Reporter **Maple Buescher,** 13, arrived at the Republican National Convention, in Cleveland, Ohio, from her nearby hometown of Cleveland Heights. She interviewed delegates and members of the press, including *CBS This Morning* co-anchor Norah O'Donnell and *New York Times* opinion writer Emma Roller. She observed the action with a Media Floor Pass. The fast-paced atmosphere was "out of this world" according to Maple, who was the youngest reporter with credentials at the convention. "Being new gives me a-whole-nother perspective on it because I really don't have anything to compare it to," Maple told a local newspaper.

## DEMOCRATIC CONVENTION
### July 25–28, 2016 ★ Philadelphia, PA

**Democratic Nominee:** Hillary Clinton

**Fame Factor:** Former First Lady, Senator of New York, and Secretary of State

**Running Mate:** Tim Kaine

**Fame Factor:** Senator of Virginia

**Convention Theme:** Stronger Together

**Platforms:** Health and human rights and equality at home and abroad

"If there are any little girls out there who stayed up late to watch, let me just say I may become the first woman president but one of you is next"

—Hillary Clinton's nomination acceptance speech

## INSIDE THE CONVENTION

Kid Reporter **Olivia Branan,** 12, traveled to the Democratic National Convention in Philadelphia, Pennsylvania, from La Mesa, California. She sat in the press gallery with *TIME* reporters, spoke to NBC journalist Kelly O'Donnell, and heard speeches from President Obama and former President Bill Clinton. Olivia's favorite experience was interviewing Texan Clarissa Rodriguez. Rodriguez was the youngest delegate at the convention. "It was truly inspiring to hear her story about how her community came together to help pay for her trip to Philadelphia," Olivia wrote in her daily log for *TIME FOR KIDS*.

# Welcome to the White House

When a new president is elected, it's time for the first family to pack up and move into the grand mansion at 1600 Pennsylvania Avenue in Washington, D.C. The White House has been home to every presidential family except George Washington's. In its rooms, our leaders have planned wars, signed important laws and treaties, welcomed foreign leaders, and made historic speeches.

Engraved view of the front facade of the White House and its grounds, 1850.

In 1790, Washington asked Congress to determine where the president's house should be built. At the time, the nation's capital was Philadelphia. But Congress had set aside a large empty section of land in which to build a new capital city. Architect James Hoban began construction of the president's new home in 1792, in a city that would eventually be named for the first president. In 1800, President John Adams and his family

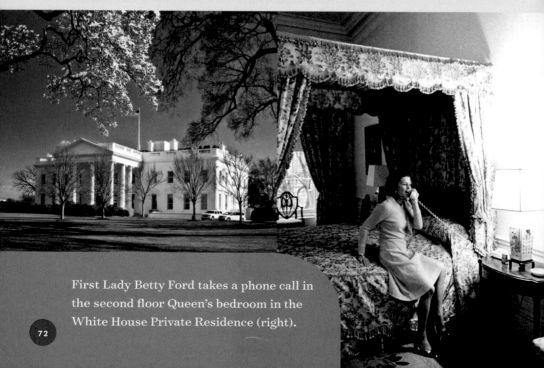

First Lady Betty Ford takes a phone call in the second floor Queen's bedroom in the White House Private Residence (right).

The Red Room of the White House, decorated for the holidays.

moved into the cold, damp, and unfinished mansion. Since then, it has survived two fires and numerous remodelings.

The home and office of the U.S. president is the only private residence of a head of state that is free and open to the public. Each year hundreds of thousands of visitors tour the White House.

First Lady Laura Bush takes Michelle Obama for a private tour of the artwork in the East Wing (Green Room) of the White House.

# The Nation's First Ladies

Martha Washington became the first wife of a U.S. president in 1789. She took on the job of being hostess to all those who came to visit the leader of the new nation. But Martha Washington preferred the quiet home life she had left behind. She said she felt like a "state prisoner." But like her husband, she believed it was her duty to serve the public.

The early first ladies were strong supporters of the American Revolution and took personal risks along with their husbands. Abigail Adams was John Adams's closest advisor. They wrote almost daily letters to each other during his many travels across the colonies and in Europe.

**Abigail Adams**

Dolley Madison acted as hostess for President Thomas Jefferson, whose wife had died. She continued hosting when her own husband became president. Madison loved being a hostess, and she became a social celebrity. During the War of 1812, Madison rescued important papers and a portrait of George Washington from the White House as the British troops invaded.

Although Dolley Madison was called "America's First Lady" at her funeral, the title didn't really catch on until Lucy Hayes's time in the White House. The presidents' wives have been "first ladies" ever since.

One of the most popular first ladies in U.S. history was Eleanor Roosevelt, the wife of Franklin D. Roosevelt. She traveled widely, met often with the press,

**First ladies: Eleanor Roosevelt, Hillary Rodham Clinton, and Laura Bush**

and wrote a daily newspaper column. Eleanor Roosevelt was a big influence on her husband. She was involved in the labor, civil rights, and women's movements, as well as shaping the New Deal economic relief plan. The press called her "First Lady of the World."

Jacqueline Kennedy brought a new level of style and culture to the White House. She helped create the center for performing arts that was later named after her husband, John F. Kennedy. The public loved "Jackie," and many women imitated the way she dressed. In 1962, she renovated the White House and gave the nation its first televised tour.

All the presidents' wives of the past four decades have taken a stand on important issues. Jackie Kennedy urged government support for the arts. Lady Bird Johnson worked to beautify the nation's highways. Betty Ford supported the passage of the Equal Rights Amendment and brought the modern women's movement into the cultural mainstream. Rosalynn Carter became an expert on policy in Latin America and supported aid for the elderly. Barbara Bush worked to end illiteracy. Laura Bush worked for education reform and the rights of women and families worldwide. Hillary Rodham Clinton was actively involved in policies shaping health care. When her husband left office, she became the only first lady who had her own political career when she was elected to the U.S. Congress as a senator from New York. She later served as secretary of state under President Barack Obama, and ran for president in 2008 and 2016. Michelle Obama's "Let's Move" initiative brought together communities in an effort to address child obesity.

**Michelle Obama**

# Presidential Gallery

Since 1789, there have been 45 presidents of the United States. Here they all are, from George Washington to Donald J. Trump.

1
★ George ★
Washington

2
★ John ★
Adams

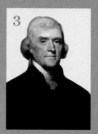
3
★ Thomas ★
Jefferson

4
★ James ★
Madison

5
★ James ★
Monroe

6
★ John Quincy ★
Adams

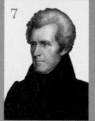
7
★ Andrew ★
Jackson

8
★ Martin ★
Van Buren

9
★ William ★
Henry Harrison

10
★ John ★
Tyler

11
★ James K. ★
Polk

12
★ Zachary ★
Taylor

13
★ Millard ★
Fillmore

14
★ Franklin ★
Pierce

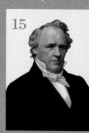
15
★ James ★
Buchanan

16
★ Abraham ★
Lincoln

17
★ Andrew ★
Johnson

18
★ Ulysses S. ★
Grant

19
★ Rutherford B. ★
Hayes

20
★ James ★
Garfield